D1130282

THE 100X
LEADER

THE 100X LEADER

HOW TO BECOME SOMEONE WORTH FOLLOWING

JEREMIE KUBICEK & STEVE COCKRAM

WILEY

Cover image: Henry Be on Unsplash

Cover design: Wiley

Copyright © 2019 by Pub House, LLC. All rights reserved.

Published by John Wiley & Sons, Inc., Hoboken, New Jersey.
Published simultaneously in Canada.

No part of this publication may be reproduced, stored in a retrieval system, or transmitted in any form or by any means, electronic, mechanical, photocopying, recording, scanning, or otherwise, except as permitted under Section 107 or 108 of the 1976 United States Copyright Act, without either the prior written permission of the Publisher, or authorization through payment of the appropriate per-copy fee to the Copyright Clearance Center, Inc., 222 Rosewood Drive, Danvers, MA 01923, (978) 750-8400, fax (978) 646-8600, or on the Web at www.copyright.com. Requests to the Publisher for permission should be addressed to the Permissions Department, John Wiley & Sons, Inc., 111 River Street, Hoboken, NJ 07030, (201) 748-6011, fax (201) 748-6008, or online at http://www.wiley.com/go/permissions.

Limit of Liability/Disclaimer of Warranty: While the publisher and author have used their best efforts in preparing this book, they make no representations or warranties with respect to the accuracy or completeness of the contents of this book and specifically disclaim any implied warranties of merchantability or fitness for a particular purpose. No warranty may be created or extended by sales representatives or written sales materials. The advice and strategies contained herein may not be suitable for your situation. You should consult with a professional where appropriate. Neither the publisher nor author shall be liable for any loss of profit or any other commercial damages, including but not limited to special, incidental, consequential, or other damages.

For general information on our other products and services or for technical support, please contact our Customer Care Department within the United States at (800) 762-2974, outside the United States at (317) 572-3993 or fax (317) 572-4002.

Wiley publishes in a variety of print and electronic formats and by print-on-demand. Some material included with standard print versions of this book may not be included in e-books or in print-on-demand. If this book refers to media such as a CD or DVD that is not included in the version you purchased, you may download this material at http://booksupport.wiley.com. For more information about Wiley products, visit www.wiley.com.

Library of Congress Cataloging-in-Publication Data:

Names: Kubicek, Jeremie, author. | Cockram, Steve, author.
Title: The 100X leader : how to become someone worth following / Jeremie
 Kubicek, Steve Cockram.
Description: Hoboken, New Jersey : John Wiley & Sons, Inc., [2019] | Includes
 index. |
Identifiers: LCCN 2018043695 (print) | LCCN 2018045132 (ebook) | ISBN
 9781119519478 (Adobe PDF) | ISBN 9781119519454 (ePub) | ISBN 9781119519447
 (hardcover)
Subjects: LCSH: Leadership.
Classification: LCC HD57.7 (ebook) | LCC HD57.7 .K81545 2019 (print) | DDC
 658.4/092–dc23
LC record available at https://lccn.loc.gov/2018043695

Printed in the United States of America

V10011634_062619

I want to dedicate this work to my dad, Mike Kubicek, who has constantly fought for my highest possible good. You are my hero and a leader worth following!
—Jeremie

For Helen, Izzy, Megan, and Charlotte—thank you for sharing this incredible adventure with me, with all my love.
—Steve

Contents

SECTION III   Creating 100X Cultures

Introduction

There is a people group on this planet known for their super-human abilities. They can climb at levels unimaginable, while carrying gear and supplies that would make the normal person wince. They are known as the Sherpa, and they are a perfect metaphor to describe a type of superhuman leader that exists on this planet as well.

You may know the Sherpa for their expertise on Mount Everest and throughout the Himalaya mountains. Even more than their physical DNA, the Sherpa tend to have a belief system that is different than the extreme climbers who pay thousands to climb a mountain, seeking mostly the thrill of personal achievement. In contrast, the Sherpa climb out of respect for the mountain and for the chance to take care of their families.

Two types of people climb the mountain for different reasons: one to check off an accomplishment, the other to help people fulfill their dreams. Throughout this book, we use the metaphor of a Sherpa because we feel they are the best example of what it means to truly lead people, modeling perfectly the ability to calibrate support and challenge. We will explain what we mean by a "100X leader" in depth and give you many practical tools and examples as we challenge you to live and lead at your full potential. Our ultimate goal is to help you become a person who people *want to* follow, not one people *have to* follow. There is a big difference.

"Have to" versus "Want to"

Have you ever worked for someone simply because you needed a job or a paycheck? This was a leader that you reluctantly worked for out of duty or necessity, but one you wouldn't necessarily have chosen to work for otherwise.

Mentally, "want to" versus "have to" is a very different thing. When we want to work for someone, life is much brighter. When we work for someone worth following, we have a spring in our step, we want to work hard. But, when we are forced to work for a weak leader, even things we like to do become tedious.

In this book we will help you evaluate how others see your leadership and your life, and we will equip you with proven practical tools so that you can become someone people will choose to follow.

We Need Better Leaders

The twenty-first century is a steep mountain climb for today's leaders; the landscape is treacherous and constantly shifting as the complexities of work, culture, and life are changing rapidly in the digital age. It's unrecognizable from 30 years ago! In essence, the terrain has changed drastically, and people are either adapting or not.

Because of these changes we have come to believe that the world doesn't need more leaders—it needs more of the right kind of leaders, especially amid the chaos that is constant within global affairs. We need more leaders who people want to believe in, not leaders who people are forced to follow.

The changes in geopolitical realities, global leadership, and technological advancements have also caused a complete shift in the way adults learn. People have changed the way they read and view information and even the way they read books. Social media affects news feeds and attitudes, not to mention the endless options of entertainment. The proliferation of information has forced different behaviors as people try to filter what they want to take in and how much content to digest, whether it's audio, visual, or text. This dramatic shift in how we learn affects people's abilities to become healthy and to train others effectively.

No one has climbed this mountain before. Having worked with leaders around the globe, we know the challenges of today's landscape. The realities that leaders are asked to address require a new technique since the old maps are invalid. Since 2013 we have been working to create new maps for twenty-first-century leaders—a people system that actually scales and multiplies healthy leaders. And it has been working, which is why we have built this field guide for transformation and multiplication for you to use.

Transformation and Multiplication Methodology

This book is written for every person who leads others in many different circles of influence—from the CEO to the director to the front-line manager to the parent at home with kids or to the leader inside a community. Our goal is to establish a new standard of leadership, one that is centered on humility, self-awareness, and excellence but also accepts the challenge to multiply other leaders with the same DNA.

You will quickly understand our philosophy and our goal to help you become as healthy a leader as possible and learn how to multiply your skills to others. Ultimately, we will take the greatest delight when your spouse, kids, teammates or employees notice a tangible difference in you and comment on it. Such stories of transformational change are our true metric of success.

We believe you cannot remove leadership from real life. You might only be leading one person—yourself—and even then, you can learn to lead more effectively. Even if you simply grow personally to a higher level of self-awareness and begin to liberate yourself, then this book is worth it. We believe passionately in applied leadership learning—we don't just want you to know more about leadership, we want you to become a leader who others are proud to follow.

Here is how one leader described the book while reading an early version:

> This book puts it all together. It helps me on my own view of myself, affects my role in my family and gives me real tools to help me with my people. You guys put the words to my thoughts and gave me something that I can use as a field guide. I honestly think I will be able to keep this book open on my desk to help me with my real life at work and at home.
> —**Brandon Hutchins, CEO, Gaskins Surveying & Engineering, Marietta, Georgia**

Where the Change Starts

But we believe that you must first change yourself before you can attempt to change others. This is the secret of the Sherpa, or 100X leader. As we help you change your view of the future, your priorities and your goals, this will create the possibility for a ripple effect that will change your families, teams, organizations, and communities.

We need leaders who lead for the benefit of others, not just for themselves.

To be a 100X leader you must be honest and challenge your core motivation:

- What do you really want?
- What do you desire to achieve by the time you are 40, 50, or 65-plus years of age?
- How are you planning to actually get there?
- What are you afraid of losing?
- Looking at your past leadership, what would others conclude was your motivation? Is it accurate? And, do you want to change that perception?

Change starts when a person "looks in a mirror" and first becomes aware that there is some blemish or tendency that needs to be addressed.

We can't change you. We can only hold up a mirror to challenge and encourage you to start the process of becoming a leader worth following.

When you finish this book, hopefully you will have accomplished two things:

1. You will have experienced a profound personal insight, a pathway, and a vision of a better way to live and lead.
2. You will start to become adept at intentionally transferring what you have learned to help others.

The 100X process is a journey. We hope this field guide will give you a new language of leadership, and that you will let us be your Sherpas to help you lead at higher levels and then have the joy of helping others climb.

Welcome to base camp. Let's get ready to become someone worth following.

SECTION 1

Developing You

1 | Choosing to Climb

On May 20, 2013 at approximately 3:30 a.m., John Beede was rudely awakened by his alarm. He had been dreaming about enjoying the most amazing cup of hot tea he had ever had, while eating some delicious warm pastries in a local cafe.

As he began to awake from his slumber he realized the awful reality that it was just a dream—a cruel dream. There was neither tea nor any scrumptious pastry, but instead he could hear the strong arctic wind that sounded like a freight train and reminded him where he was. It was the type of wind that threatens climbers not to go any further. As he began to stir, the extreme cold seeped into his sleeping bag and snapped him to reality. This was the day—the day he would remember for the rest of his life. If he made it back to tell about it.

Nestled at 23,500 feet at Camp 3 on Mount Everest, after 45 days on the mountain, nine months of training and 17 years of dreaming it was time for John to start the final leg of his journey.

John is an expert climber and one of the few who have climbed the seven summits—the highest single mountain on each of the seven continents. In his life he has climbed over 100 mountains, but only one remained—the most magnificent mountain on earth, Mount Everest. And the mountain held all his respect.

Just like the morning rituals of the Sherpa, John prepared his mind in the few minutes he had before dressing and leaving for this important feat. This morning, like every other morning, he listened to a talk about mind over matter from a motivational speaker and then read a few messages from family to inspire him for what he was about to do.

John had prepared physically and he was in the best shape of his life, though the time on Everest was beginning to take its toll. He was ready for summit day. He had perfected the technical aspects of climbing and could manage ropes and his climbing tools with the best of them. His focus was on his emotional and mental endurance. He would have to handle the negative voices in his head and the ramifications of other people cracking under the sheer emotional, mental, and physical stress of climbing in the death zone.

Oh yeah, the death zone. That is the roughly 3,000 feet of mountain from Camp 4 to the summit that is the most treacherous terrain on the planet. This is the altitude where airplanes fly and where the oxygen needed for life just doesn't exist. Each climber has less than 48 hours to climb from Camp 4 to the summit and back down to Camp 3 (see Figure 1.1). In fact, the year of John's climb, nine people died in Everest's death zone. Through his binoculars, John watched one climber perish attempting a climb. He would see six other dead bodies in all as he climbed, a devastating blow to the psyche of even a world-class climber.

Figure 1.1   John Beede's ascent to the summit of Mount Everest.
Source: **Courtesy of www.alanarnette.com© reproduction prohibited without authorization.**

They reached Camp 4 at 26,300 feet by 11 a.m. for a rest. Can you imagine resting in the death zone? Though the rest helped, every climber was focused on the final push to the summit that started at 7 p.m.

The first steps out of Camp 4 committed John into the blackness of the frozen Himalayan night sky. The next 30 hours would mark the culminating moments of a 17-year mountaineering and climbing career. This was his final "testing ground" of self-discovery and personal growth. Since the mountain wasn't about to lower itself to his level, it was his opportunity to rise up to the demands presented by the climb.

John pondered to himself, "Do I have what it takes? Could I perform at my best in the most extreme environment on earth? Can I balance my skills, physical strength, emotional endurance, teamwork, and safety judgments?" Step after grueling step, the truth sunk in to him. John thought, "every person needs his or her own personal proving place; this is mine."

That night would be one of the most intense of John's life. The only comfort was that he was not alone. Nuru, one of the most coveted Sherpa guides, had climbed right beside him since base camp, and together they reevaluated the weather for the right window to summit.

Each climber was given two canisters of oxygen along the way, one in the beginning and one stored higher, both supposed to last 10 hours each—enough to take them from Camp 3 to the summit and back down safely to Camp 2. John, however, had an issue with his oxygen. His first canister only lasted 3 hours, not 10. An oxygen canister is threaded like the cap of a screw top bottle, and the rubber threads on John's tank began to warp from the extreme cold, failing to seal properly, causing the oxygen to leak.

Nuru, his Sherpa, did what he was trained to do—he climbed higher to get the other fresh tank that was stored for the upper levels so that they could continue the climb. As John waited, the colors around him began to fade. His red coat became gray as his eyes began to shut down due to lack of oxygen. Nuru returned in the nick of time.

The new oxygen tank took him as far as the Hillary step, but no further. The extreme cold caused the oxygen to leak on this tank as well. He was out of time and was advised to turn back. The most frustrating part was that John could hear climbers celebrating the summit just meters away from him. He was just too close to give up. His Sherpa tried a serendipitous last resort fix, as he dipped John's canister into a container of hot tea to melt the ice and make a seal. John's dream of hot tea, which had begun at the break of day, now gave him just enough oxygen to get to the next level. He eventually reached the summit at 5:48 a.m. on May 21, 2013, a testament to his courage and to the ingenuity and wisdom of his Sherpa (see Figure 1.2). He is one of the few who have braved the weather and faced death with every step to make it through the death zone and back to do what very few on the planet have ever done—summit Mount Everest.

Mount Everest is not for everyone, and many people in a climbing group don't make it to the top. Although John Beede did make it, he explains that the two months of preparation and climbing on the mountain can wear people down. "Most people don't realize that you have to attempt Mount Everest three to four times before making it to the top to acclimate your body." There is no way your body would make it without this acclimation strategy. He says, "The

Figure 1.2 John Beede with his Sherpa, Nuru, at the summit of Mount Everest.
Source: **Photo courtesy of John Beede.**

people who are strongest physically don't always make it, but rather it is the emotionally strong, the ones who can work as a team and are willing to help others, who seem to thrive." More than anything, he emphasized, a successful climb depended on the experience and quality of the Sherpa as guide. John is still climbing mountains and spends the rest of his time speaking to leaders on how to live and lead in the midst of obstacles.

Aiming Higher

Our goal for this book is to help you climb your own leadership Mount Everest—whether that be to lead a team, run a division or a company, or raise a family at a higher level. We want you to aim higher in your view of yourself and those you lead. We want to be your Sherpas on a journey of intentional living, to help you be the best leader in all the spheres of influence in your life. And, we want you in turn to learn how to become a Sherpa for others. We aim to get you to a place of 100% health and influence, which means we need to help you acclimate to higher levels on your journey of growth and self-awareness before effectively leading others up their mountains.

100X

So, how do we get you to 100% health in your leadership, and is it even possible? We want to introduce you to a symbol that can be used by you inside your world to help shape the intent of people becoming healthy leaders. That symbol is 100X.

The phrase 100X is simple and deep all at the same time. The number 100 simply means reaching 100% of the desired health or personal transformation of a person, encompassing their emotional intelligence, mental ability, and holistic leadership strength and effectiveness.

The hallmarks of a leader at 100% could look like the following:

- They are secure in who they are and confident with their abilities while remaining humble to those they serve.
- They are consistent in the way they lead so that people can count on them.
- They are self-aware and responsive when they have erred.
- They are intently for their people, not against them, or solely for themselves.
- They have something to give others because they are full of the positive even in the midst of difficult circumstances.

Although 100% is rarely reached, the aspiration of being as healthy as a leader can be should be your goal—the ability to know yourself and lead yourself in order to be the most effective person/leader possible. The leadership journey is similar to that which John Beede experienced with Nuru, his Sherpa. We are simply your guides, focused on helping you become the consistent, healthy leader you would love to be. This journey, like climbing the highest mountain, will help you acclimate at higher levels of living and leading. Some of the exercises in this guidebook will make you feel like you don't have much oxygen as we encourage you to face yourself and your tendencies in order to push you higher, but if you commit to getting truly healthy and allow the process to do its work, you are going to find yourself climbing at levels that were once unattainable.

And the X in 100X? The X stands for multiplication—the intentional transfer of knowledge, wisdom, and skills to those you lead. Once you journey up the mountain yourself and prove that you have what it takes, you will become the Sherpa for those you lead.

Put together, 100X is a formula for leadership success—transformation of the leader and multiplication to those you lead. Some of you might be at 70%, as you are generally healthy in your leadership, but may not be multiplying or helping others climb in the way they need. We are inviting you to climb Everest every day for the rest of your lives and learn how to be a Sherpa to others at the same time.

Become, Build, Lead

To do that well, you will need to become well rounded in three fundamental areas of your life. You will need to:

1. Become a leader worth following, not one people must follow because of a job or just because you are their boss.
2. Build leaders worth following because every organization needs much stronger leaders to be able to sustain and grow.
3. Lead organizations (or cultures) that people want to join. People have a choice and we will help you create teams and organizations that people want to attach their names to.

We have seen too much—too many leaders who are focused on their own leadership but have given very little to helping others win. We have also seen the leaders who decimate everyone they lead. We will address this as well.

In *The 100X Leader* you will experience a holistic view of becoming a person that people want to follow. To get there, we must jump in to real life and work on real issues that might be hard, but will certainly be good.

Leaders in Real Life

Every one of us has our realities that we must live with every day. We have partners, bosses, marriages, kids, friend-ships, clients, and more to navigate through on a daily basis. Throughout the book we will be sharing many real-life stories of transformation and multiplication as we attempt to show a better way to live and lead.

Dan O'Berski is an amazing leader. He is a successful real estate developer in Estero, Florida. Years ago, he made the decision to go on the 100X journey after observing the transformation from a friend who had experienced our process. When Dan first met us, his leadership health was around 70% because he didn't fully know what it was like to be on the other side of his leadership. Here is how he tells it.

By 2011 we had started a new company and when we started, my tendencies and patterns were to overcome obstacles by sheer determination and activity. We had grown the company from 4 people to 12 in two years and believed we were on the right track, though along the way there were a growing number of casualties. I would cast the vision to anyone that would hear me out and I would communicate the future as if it was a guaranteed reality. This led to unrealistic expectations on how we would get to our future with a group of young and motivated individuals that were trying to read my mind on how to actually get to that vision daily.

I truly cared about these people and wanted to see them accomplish their dreams (which of course would aid my dreams), but there were so many problems— mainly with me. I found myself exhausted from doing all the work they couldn't do and getting increasingly frustrated with the team when we didn't reach our goals. I would press them to the point of threatening to fire them or actually releasing them.

My leadership wasn't healthy and I definitely was multiplying the wrong things. This caused people to see me as a tyrant at times. It seemed to me that everyone was lazy and no one wanted it, as much as I did, which I know now wasn't truly fair. I probably appeared to be highly successful. The reality was, I was not providing the support or the challenge that was needed for any reasonably hardworking person to reach the outcome I desired.

I made a decision to change. I chose to find people to help me, to act as a Sherpa to help me reach a higher level of leading. They provided me with tools and trained me to use those tools to climb. I'm still not 100%, but I am above an 85% and I know what I need to do to get even higher. I have also started to multiply myself and I realize that I learn even more about myself when I help others grow. To become a Sherpa yourself and get to 100X is the hardest challenge I have ever taken, but I am never going back down the mountain.

The journey contained in this book is full of hope, and some surprises, as we hold up a mirror to let you see what it's like to be on the other side of you. There is a summit awaiting you with the most incredible view, when you let the process of self-discovery have its way.

Your 100% Health Check

To make the most of the rest of the book, prepare for the journey by taking a quick, unscientific, reality health check for your life now. Rank yourself 1–10 (10 being the highest level of health) on each of these statements.

- I am secure, not insecure, in my ability to lead people, teams, programs, or organizations to accomplish our goals. 1–10 _____
- My personal life is healthy and allows me to be fully present and productive in accomplishing my objectives and goals. 1–10 _____
- I am emotionally intelligent and have acclimated to leadership by learning how to lead people in complex situations. 1–10 _____
- I am consistent in my leadership and not prone to rash emotions or using fear and manipulation to lead others. 1–10 _____
- I know where I am going and what I am responsible for and feel the freedom and courage to lead at higher levels. 1–10 _____
- I am fit to lead, physically, mentally, and emotionally. 1–10 _____

Now, average your scores and divide by six. A score of 7 and above would highlight that you believe you are in a healthy season. A score of 5 and under would mean that there are real issues happening in your life and that you need some help to get healthy enough to continue climbing. Lastly, if you are between 5 and 7 then there are some flags that need to be addressed, as you could easily move up or down based on some circumstances in your life.

100% is the goal. Most of us are not at that number as stress and pressure, missed expectations, hard relational dynamics, kids, and life in general have shaved this number down into something well below. We believe that once you go through the gauntlet of Chapters 2, 3, and 4 that this number could go lower through the realities of self-awareness. And, we also believe that we will help you get to the next level as you begin to work on yourself and acclimate to the higher levels of living and leading.

As Sherpas, we will make sure we help you get to where you have wanted to go but didn't know how. In the last chapter we will then give you a scientific way to fully analyze your reality and see your true number.

Acknowledging Your Journey to Date

We all have things in our past that have hammered and shaped us into the person we are in this moment. Because we are complex and layered, it is often hard to reflect deeper on your life, but it is important to take a look inside so that you can work on the outside.

One question we love to ask is, "What are the things that have caused you to stop being you?" Here is another, "What is keeping you from being fully alive, healthy, and ready to climb?" Such questions are designed to provoke thoughts that could lead to transformation, as growth is a process, a journey that takes years, even decades.

If you want to know how a leader will act or predict the decisions they will make, you need only look backward to find the people, circumstances, and decisions that shaped them in the past, whether positive or negative, to be the person they are today.

We believe that people become the conversations of those around them, and many of us are culminations of the comments and expectations of others in our life. This book will help frame a better narrative so that you can climb your own mountain.

It Always Starts with You

Here is an extreme story from one of our clients who went through the 100X process and rated himself below 20% in overall health as a leader and a person. The truth is that we cannot become Sherpas—100X leaders—until we become healthy ourselves and have learned how to live in that health. A Sherpa who isn't healthy is a person who is not helpful to others trying to get to the next level. They become a liability rather than a resource for the other person.

Todd found himself knotted up on the floor, wrapped up in his eight-year-old daughter's Hello Kitty blanket. He didn't know if he was having a heart attack or a meltdown. For the past 20 years Todd had led a nonprofit that helps turn troubled boys into transformed young men. It was ironic that Todd was now in trouble.

In his words, "What I was experiencing had caught me totally off guard. In reality, this wreckage had been set in motion at least 48 months prior. I was not sleeping at night. My heart raced. I felt overwhelming anxiety. I had lost over 40 pounds. I never felt rested and seldom experienced peace or joy. I was constantly in work mode trying to solve the issues of our nonprofit. That is what you do as a founder, I thought. I was present physically with my family. However, emotionally I might as well have been half way around the world as I was consumed on helping everyone else except me."

When Todd finally came for help, he was overly responsible, controlled by guilt and insecurities. He was responsible for donors, the board, the staff, and ultimately the kids. Most of his work appeared healthy, even admirable, as he served so many. What most didn't know, however, was that Todd was dying on the inside and had nothing to multiply.

This is a key point: you can't give what you don't possess. Todd didn't have anything to give. He was depleted and he needed a change. He began filling his time and mind with the start of the EOTE Coffee Company, which is now one of the fastest growing coffee brands in the industry. His way of life was not healthy or sustainable and his crash was entirely inevitable.

You can't give what you don't possess.

Todd shares,

> Two weeks after my Hello Kitty crash, I was in Jeremie's office where I came face to face with the habits and tendencies that were killing me. Even though I had a master's degree in counseling, I realized that I needed help to get healthy. I was at 20% at best and had nothing to give to others. Who I really was and what I had adapted and learned to do as a founder of an organization were two different things. I was exhausted and insecure. I was trying to be someone I was not. That day was the turning point in my life. I realized that I could no longer operate the same way that I had done my entire adult life.

Over the next 24 months, we took Todd on a journey of liberation and transformation. Todd needed oxygen, and so we had to go to a lower camp to get him healthy before he could begin to climb the mountain again. First, he had to rest, both emotionally and physically. Dramatic changes had to be made. Todd resigned as CEO of the nonprofit and focused on his health and his work at EOTE Coffee. We helped him reset his whole outlook, giving him a new language, tools, and concepts contained later in this book.

As Todd summarizes,

> I feel liberated! I am now healthy again and I have come to know my tendencies and patterns so that I can lead myself. When I learn my triggers, I can operate out of truth rather than fear. When I operate out of my strengths, I am confident, energized, and live out of my competencies rather than out of my insecurities. I have been given the tools and language to help me get healthy as a leader. It's also had a ripple effect throughout my marriage, family, career, and my community.

Multiplication is not the priority when you are not healthy! Personal transformation is a prerequisite for intentionally transferring what you know to others.

Preclimb Checklist

We want you, like Todd, to experience the summit—to experience the joy and satisfaction of leading at higher levels and, in time, guiding others up the summit. Here are our Sherpa recommendations to outfit you for the summit:

- Use the tools that we provide you to increase your self-awareness. Get ready to really know yourself well— the good, the bad, the ugly.
- Get to the root of your personal tendencies and patterns as you become a leader worth following.

- Review your past, especially the positive and negative influences in your life.
- Ask yourself this question: "How have I passed on the negative influences of my life into the lives of others?" And the positive influences?
- Remind yourself of times when your positive influence has had good results and put those actions on your "keep doing" list. Keep track of what works and what doesn't.
- Put in the time needed for you to acclimate, knowing that you are going to go up and down the mountain before you can lead at the higher levels of a 100X leader to become, build, and lead.

We must all come to terms with the fact that we are who we are. But although we can't change our yesterdays, we can absolutely affect today and tomorrow, if only we are intentional on our journey.

Where to Go from Here

Most people never even make it to base camp, lacking the resources or the motivation to improve. Those who decide to get to the next level must first make their own journey of self-awareness, while getting to 100% health, as the first climb. The X climb of multiplication comes later.

Because the journey to 100% is the first climb, you must work to become more secure, confident, and humble as a leader along the way. This is not just about you becoming a better person or crafting the life you want for yourself; you influence far too many people throughout your life to make it solely about you. It's about you not just climbing the mountain, but becoming a Sherpa to those you lead.

2 | The Making of a Sherpa

The metaphor of a Sherpa perfectly connects with the vision we have of the 100X leader. It is a person who is acclimated to the mountain, because they have climbed it so many times themselves and they are now healthy enough to climb easily up and down to help other people summit for the first time.

Born at the highest levels of the Himalayas, the Sherpa, meaning "coming from the East," are a people group that live in altitudes and temperatures that would cause most of us to faint. Intimately connected with their religion and world-view, the Sherpa people have many rituals and rites of passage along with a deep reverence for the mountains. Although they must manage the technical aspects of mountaineering, rope management, and emergency descents, as well as technical oxygen requirements, they simply have the unfair advantage of years of advanced acclimation!

It could also be said that the maker of the Sherpa is the mountain itself. The altitude forces the expansion of the lungs from the Sherpa's first breath; the stories told by older climbers become their first memories. The mountain, with all its intricacies, is the trainer to the Sherpa. In the same way, the leadership journey—in the office, dealing with the team—is the trainer of the leader. It isn't the seminar or the book that makes the difference but the atmosphere where leadership gets forced into action and the applied leadership learning that happens on the spot.

Becoming a Sherpa

The Sherpa people are a Tibetan ethnic group who live predominantly in the highest altitudes in the world—the Himalayas. This genetic predisposition of altitude acclimation has given them the reputation of being some of the best mountain climbers in the world.

The Sherpa on Mount Everest have grown up on or around the mountain. The Sherpa call it "Chomolungma" and respect the mountain as the "Mother of the World." In an attitude of reverence, they work to help climbers hit the highest target in the world. The truth about Sherpa is that they are devoted to helping each other and serving their clients to the highest level.

Unless you are born a Sherpa, you cannot truly become one, as you must be born into that tribe and tradition. However, metaphorically speaking, to become a Sherpa is attainable in the leadership context. A Sherpa in this context is someone who has climbed his own mountain, learned how to lead himself and can thrive in higher altitudes, all the while helping other people climb up the same mountain. Figuratively speaking, the making of a Sherpa is the making of the 100X leader who must learn all of the technical aspects of leading, from communications to performance management to alignment and execution to dealing with people on every level. Our objective then is to develop fully acclimated leaders who, like the Sherpa, can move up and down the mountain while helping others move up themselves. Here are some key attributes of the 100X leader we are espousing with the end goal of developing leaders who lead people effectively:

- They must decide that they want to become someone worth following and want to learn the secrets to becoming one of the best leaders in the world.
- They must become self-aware, knowing who they are and why they do what they do and be willing to change those patterns and actions for the benefit of all.
- They must learn how to calibrate support and challenge as they fight for the highest possible good of those they lead.
- As they learn to be consistent leaders, they must learn to handle hard realities and adjust as they go.
- They must desire accountability and be teachable— humble enough to let others help them up to the next level.
- They are committed to a lifelong process of intentional self-improvement.
- They must overcome the arrogance that comes from pride and learn to create a culture of empowerment and growth in the midst of turmoil and drama.

These are but a few of the things that the 100X leader must do. Since it's no longer about them and their personal achievements the 100X leader learns to take delight in the achievements of those they lead, seeing others achieve things that they never thought possible.

The Greek historian and general Thucydides once wrote, "The secret to happiness is freedom. The secret to freedom is courage." The 100X journey is a personal journey of liberation, of freedom, and it certainly takes courage—the courage to invest in yourself and what is most important in your life, the courage to do difficult things that are contrary to your natural tendencies, the courage to hold up the mirror and take a hard look at what others see and wish you would do something about, the courage to make the subtle changes you view as insignificant but are likely the most important to others, the courage to stay at it when the positive results seem slow to come. The world is badly in need of better leaders in every city, sector, and corner of organizations.

Daily courage is the path to freedom and ultimately to the happiness that comes from liberating yourself and everyone around you. Becoming a 100X leader is not something that you *have* to do as most people choose to take the easy route. There is not a lot of peer pressure to become a Sherpa because of the difficulties that come with it. However, where there is risk there is certainly reward.

Ryan Underwood, CEO of TEAMTRI, shares his 100X journey:

> I'm not going to sugar coat it, the journey of liberation to become a 100X leader is a hard climb and I'm glad for that. In the difficulty comes extreme self-awareness and if you choose to go deeper in understanding yourself, you and those who live with you are going to be glad that you did.

As I have become more self-aware, I have realized what it is like to be on the other side of me—the good and the bad. Now I've been able to formalize the good things so they can be repeated and scaled by others, which makes my team better. And, most importantly, I've been able to apologize, reconcile and put in some triggers to help me lead myself so I don't undermine my influence. I have been transformed and others have experienced it. Now I'm learning to take others through the process and I am seeing their transformation as well. I am now waking up each day climbing the mountain to get to the next level and the views are even better than they were the day before!

This journey up the mountain takes time, patience, and perseverance to realize. Grand endeavors don't happen overnight. Many leaders get close to the 100% part, but very few of them ever go on to become multipliers. Why? There are so very few examples of others doing it. Most traditional leaders have already received the plaudits for being a successful leader because of some success they may have had, and they are loved by their communities but are not taking anyone else up the mountain.

For a 100X leader who runs a large organization or has been leading a team for a long time, it can take many years to see a breakthrough in those you lead.

But, where there is good leadership, people long to be part of that culture. Families grow and communities thrive. Since leaders define culture, 100X leaders bring people, families, teams, and organizations to life.

One of the keys to becoming a 100X leader is the leader's mindset because it is crucial for you to overcome yourself if you want to lead at the higher levels. In the following

100X leaders bring people, families, teams, and organizations to life.

section we will train you to overcome your limiting beliefs so that you can help yourself and others grow.

How to Overcome Your Inhibitions

Being *prohibited* is to be told you cannot do something by someone else who has authority. Being *inhibited* is you telling yourself that you cannot do something (see Figure 2.1).

Have you ever heard someone say, "Well I tried, but they told me that I couldn't." Who are "they"? Most people think they are prohibited when they are actually inhibited. A recent example of this happened when one of our teammates didn't do something I thought we had all agreed to be done. When I

WHO SAYS YOU CAN'T?

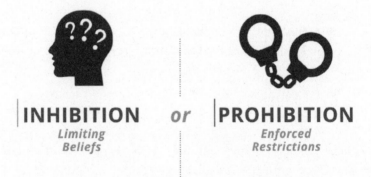

 GiANT WORLDWIDE   © Pub House

Figure 2.1 The difference between inhibition and prohibition.
Source: © **Pub House/GiANT Worldwide.**

asked why they didn't finish it, the answer was, "I thought you wouldn't want us to do that." This employee thought they were prohibited when they were actually inhibited out of fear of messing up the project.

We find that the majority of people are inhibited rather than prohibited. There are actually very few things we are really prohibited from doing. At times this can create a victim mentality that can limit people dramatically. Here is how you can ensure you are not inhibiting yourself:

- First, ask clarifying questions of others to see if you are truly prohibited from performing a task.
- Second, if you find that you are inhibiting yourself, ask yourself why.
- Finally, think through the ramifications of not doing something you should just because you are inhibited.

Refuse to think of yourself with a victim mentality. Rise above your own fears and begin to take initiative where you would normally be inhibited. You will be glad you did.

Inhibition is a default position for everyone. All of us can be inhibited to act on the dreams and visions that could lead to a greater future. However, left untouched, inhibitions can be a dangerous reality. To be inhibited is to be limited and limited is never a way to live or to lead.

We are all carrying inhibitions caused by words and opinions that have been spoken to us in our past.

Ben was told his entire life that he was stupid by his family and lived most of his life not believing he could obtain a college degree. This verbal abuse led to Ben believing he was prohibited by his own weakness to do something that he believed was needed, but out of reach. In truth, he allowed himself to become what was spoken over him. His inhibition almost caused him to miss out on a certification that would advance his life.

You can't become a 100X leader if you aren't prepared to deal honestly with your inhibitions and the words from your past that are holding you back from fulfilling your potential. And being concerned with what others think can seriously rob us of amazing feats. That is ludicrous. The mission and message inside us is much bigger than the impression of a few people.

Are you inhibited? If so, where are you limiting yourself?

What are your current inhibitions in your personal mindset (self)?

1. _____

2. _____

3. _____

4. _____

What are your current inhibitions inside your marriage and/or family?

1. _____

2. _____

3. _____

4. _____

What are your current inhibitions in your leadership inside your team or organization?

1. _____

2. _____

3. _____

4. _____

What is the cost of allowing these inhibitions to be in your life? Usually, it is in opportunity cost; because you are self-limiting, you are costing yourself time, freedom, or money.

What is your plan to unshackle yourself from your own limits? Are you inhibiting yourself from your desired goals? If you are, then you are a victim of yourself. The fear in you is keeping you from the best in you.

The fear in you is keeping you from the best in you.

Dealing with Self-Preservation

Every person who climbs has to deal with fear. The same is true for those who learn to lead at higher levels. For climbers, it is the fear of death or immobilization from altitude sickness or other hazards that tend to hold people back. There is a natural self-preservation that we all have as we manage risk and reward. However, when the fear of losing begins to control the mind and behavior, it can create deadly consequences.

Self-preservation, in summary, can be assessed by three power questions, as shown in Figure 2.2.

The Sherpas on the mountain must deal with the fear of loss and become comfortable using their experience with handling people and themselves at high levels. In the same way, the 100X leader must lean on their experiences and make difficult decisions that affect people's lives. They must

SELF-PRESERVATION

1. **What am I afraid of losing?**
2. **What am I trying to hide?**
3. **What am I trying to prove? To whom?**

RELATIONSHIP

INFLUENCE
IMPACT

GiANT WORLDWIDE   © Pub House

Figure 2.2   Three Power Questions for Self-Preservation
Source: © **Pub House/GiANT Worldwide.**

become confident in their skills and overcome each of these
self-preservation issues.[1]

> **What are you afraid of losing?** Your position and the
> salary and benefits that come with it? We deal with dozens
> of these leaders at any point in time who are so afraid of
> losing that they tend to lose themselves. In fact, in a recent
> coaching session with a CEO, he shared that just the fear of
> his board and investors seeing him fail to turn a company
> around caused his wife to separate from him because he
> overworked to such a degree that he was not present with
> the family. He eventually resigned, losing the respect he was
> working so hard to keep in the industry. Fear. The fear of
> losing can drive people to do irrational things.
> **What are you trying to hide?** The self-aware leader
> can answer any challenge without fear, while the insecure

leader will do anything to keep people from seeing their weakness. One example of this came in an honest conversation with a well-known thought leader. This leader was honest enough to admit that he was not really a good organizational leader and was tired of telling himself he really was. Instead, he came to accept that he really was a great thought leader on certain topics, but not as good at leading people. He came to the realization of what everyone else already knew. His solution was to turn the business over to two or three colleagues who were amazing leaders of people, but didn't have his skills of communication and innovation. Thanks to his increased self-awareness, everyone was liberated.

What are you trying to prove? In order to acclimate to the highest levels of leadership, this question must be dealt with honestly. Many leaders fall down along the way while trying to prove to others that they are strong. Mike Oppedahl, our managing partner at GiANT, shares the story of a younger leader who was trying to prove that he belonged in the CEO seat to the board of directors that placed him in that role. Mike states, "It was crazy, his insecurity led him to constantly prove his worth to the board that hired him. He was constantly sending out reports that made him look good and hiding the reports that could cause any doubts. It didn't fool anyone." This is classic self-preservation.

Put another way, self-preservation is the overprotection of what you are afraid of losing. When you overprotect you tend to lose what you were afraid of losing in the first place.

What are you trying to prove and to whom? Is it your board or business partners or administration or simply your boss? Proving yourself is a natural rite of passage in any job. You want to do a good job so that people have confidence in you. However, if insecurity is rooted deeply in you, then the overproving can actually cause an undermining that can affect your influence and your respect.

When you overprotect you tend to lose what you were afraid of losing in the first place.

To climb to the higher levels on the 100X journey, we need to break through our own insecurities to become secure, confident, and humble people.

Breakthrough

A breakthrough is defined as a sudden, dramatic, and important discovery or development. Moving onto the next level will always mean working through this type of discovery for yourself in your journey of self-awareness.

Here is how a school administrator got to her breakthrough:

> I remember the day and time of my breakthrough. I learned I had become someone in such deep self-preservation that I had changed who I was as a leader and not to the good. Several years ago, a senior boy abused two kindergarten students on my watch as a school leader. Before this situation I would say that I was adept at liberating others. I was never afraid as I empowered teams of teachers and community members to do what was best for their students. I led with my heart and had deep relationships with people. I was a strong communicator and took risks for kids and teachers to make things better. We were on the cutting edge. My vision was strong and I believed there wasn't anything we couldn't do.

But after the horrific event of the abuse, my sense of responsibility—feeling I had failed to protect them—led me to believe I was a catastrophic disappointment to everyone. Because of this I lost my confidence and grew insecure. I moved into self-preservation, assuming I could be fired at any time. I stopped being a liberator and started doing what everyone told me to do. I stopped leading the way I had always led and left my job.

I was lucky enough to have a job open in my hometown and was hired back by them even though I felt I was damaged goods. I felt I needed to be hard-hitting to please my new boss. I did as I was told, aimed to please, stopped thinking about bringing liberation to people, and just got the work done at all costs, over-anxious to keep my job. None of us liked the hard culture and the ship gradually started to sink. My boss left, and the new leader sidelined me.

I was ready to move on again. I really didn't know who I was anymore, where I fit in and I sunk deeper into self-preservation mode. Then came a leadership cohort with my GiANT Sherpa, Dr. Joe Hill. I suddenly started to understand myself. I saw how my self-protecting tendencies had developed and the real me began to re-emerge. Regaining my confidence and security has been the hardest. Valuing myself has been the second hardest.

I am moving back into the liberating phase of my career. I have found my voice and I have started using it. I am not afraid anymore. I have found the peace I need to lead again the way I know best. I have rebuilt relationships that I have missed. I have been blessed that people have forgiven me too.

—Suraya Driscoll, Director of Learning, East Grand Forks, MN

Putting It Together

The mountain itself helps a climber become better; it functions as a teacher. We learn so much about ourselves when we start to help others climb. Whenever we teach a tool to someone and share what we have learned, the growth begins. The learning that takes place on the mountain is far greater than that read in a book or at a seminar. The Sherpa is born into a tribe in their village, but becomes a true Sherpa on the mountain by helping others summit. In the same way, the leadership journey helps a leader become a 100X leader if they are intentional, with eyes wide open, about the improvement that is actually happening in the process. Otherwise, the leadership journey eats a leader up and relegates him or her to being a poor leader with little influence.

Rich, a leader in London, allowed the mountain to shape him into becoming someone people want to follow. Hear him in his own words as he has worked to become a 100X leader:

> I recognized that my own ambition was leading me to dominate myself; I was pushing harder and harder and not paying anywhere near enough attention to my own well-being. This driven nature was bringing high challenge into my marriage, but I was giving little support to my wife. The pressure I was feeling led to me abdicating as a team leader, simply driving ahead with my own priorities and failing to give them enough of my time, which caused me to have a reputation as a dominating leader inside the organization. I was getting burned up in the process of trying to get results.
>
> Thankfully I was able to work all this out through a long process of self-awareness and patience from those around me. When the breakthrough happened, people began to notice that I was a different person. They noticed that I

went up the mountain and died a bit to my natural patterns and began to focus on liberating others. That has made all the difference as I am now focused on helping others get up the mountain and to the next level. That is what a 100X leader does.

Getting to 100% or close to it is not impossible.

Leading others up the mountain is not impossible either.

The 100X lifestyle is accessible to the intentional leader with the right intent. As we move into the climbing phase it is important to understand the cost and the upside. Is the prize worth the price? If you want to become a 100X leader you can, but it won't happen by accident and you can't make the journey alone.

Counting the Cost

Before anyone climbs Mount Everest they must understand the cost of climbing—mentally, physically, financially. The same is true for leaders who want to be intentional. It takes time and, like working out at the gym, it's not always fun, but the results are outstanding on the way to 100%. As we close this section, reflect on the liberation process for this leader from Houston, Texas who is on his way to becoming a Sherpa:

I am still on my journey to become a 100X leader. I can tell you that I am more aware of my reality, tendencies, and the consequences of my decisions as I lead myself through this self-awareness process. Learning to become intentional has been a huge factor in my progression to be a better professional, husband, father, and person. I think about this on a daily basis and how being intentional with whatever is on my agenda at work or at home is such a powerful tool in each area of life. Having made so much progress on myself, I feel that I am now ready to start focusing on multiplying my learning to my direct reports. I can really see how this process is helping me to become a "100X Leader" and others can see it too.

—**Clay Kofron, Regional Director, Gulf Coast LTC Partners**

This is the making of a Sherpa, and that is our goal for each one of you.

Note

1. Jeremie Kubicek, *Making Your Leadership Come Alive (Leadership Is Dead)* (New York: Howard/Simon & Schuster, 2011).

3 | Your Ultimate Test

"I couldn't believe what I was seeing," said Eddie Backler. "One night on top of the mountain we were sitting in a circle trying to keep warm by a small fire. Just then our Sherpa, Jangbhu, scooped up hot coals in his hands to bring them closer to each of us to keep us warm."

Eddie Backler, CEO of the Charles White Company, a property development company in Edinburgh, Scotland, was on a climb of the Mera Peak in 2009. At 19,000 feet, in the shadow of Mount Everest, Eddie and three other climbers put their faith in the hands of Jangbhu Sherpa who had summited Everest nine times before. Jangbhu quickly captured their respect as they were testing their limits like never before. "We knew he had the wherewithal to get us up the mountain, because the Sherpa was the key to our success," said Eddie. He goes on to share his experience: "Jangbhu knew what we needed before we did. He knew how to be ahead of us and when to be behind us. It is a real skill. He could read our team and get us to work together without us knowing it. He was assessing us constantly because he had to get us ready for the next levels. And while he could be quite stern, we totally knew he was for us."

Eddie went on to share how Jangbhu Sherpa was so intentional with resourcing the team with the proper food and gear and had a clear plan of attack to climb the mountain. Jangbhu created the trust that all four of them could summit and would do so.

Eddie went on to share, "Jangbhu wasn't a servant we had hired, but rather a fighter for our best. He brought challenge with support. He showed us how to climb the ice cliffs and he pushed us to do things we didn't think we could do on our own. He would say, 'you do your bit and I will do mine.' He would carry our bags when we needed it and would push us to do it ourselves when we needed it. Our Sherpa understood when to push us and when to help us, which was key. And because of that balance and his consistency we trusted him and respected him for who he was."

The Sherpa help people do what they don't believe they can do. Their secret to helping climbers lies in their ability to provide challenge commensurate to their support.

The Sherpa help people do what they don't believe they can do. Their secret to helping climbers lies in their ability to provide challenge commensurate to their support.

More Support or More Challenge?

Leading people well, consistently, over time, is one of the most difficult things to do in life. Leading people well in difficult circumstances is significantly more difficult. Especially when you know they need to get to a higher level but they cannot yet see it themselves.

Leading ourselves well, consistently, over time, can be just as difficult as leading others, especially with the numerous obligations that come with life and work. Family obligations, demanding roles, friendships, busy schedules, and on and on.

To become a person worth following is a balancing act, part science, part art. It is the calibration of managing support and challenge consistently with those you lead as well as with yourself. Most leaders default to their natural tendency of oversupport or too much challenge because they tend to live accidentally or out of habit. The Sherpa understands the objective and helps guide people using both support and challenge based on the needs of the moment to get their people to the next level.

Leadership is the calibration of support and challenge in order to help those you lead achieve their objectives or tasks that help the team or organization to win.

> *Leadership is the calibration of support and challenge in order to help those you lead achieve their objectives or tasks that help the team or organization to win.*

Ronald Heifetz, a professor at Harvard University, discusses the realities of overly challenging leadership in his work on adaptive leadership: "It's often thought that leaders are dominant within an organization and want to use their strong personalities to impose their will. This hierarchical top-down leadership style hasn't worked for a long time. It hinders the flow of information in companies, undermining cooperation and unity between teams and departments."[1]

A Sherpa understands that to maximize influence, you must practice both support and challenge and then learn how to calibrate these with each different person on your team. The same is true with any person or leader. Learning to manage your own personality tendencies and adapt to other people's patterns is a key to leadership success.

Support means to provide the appropriate help others need to do their jobs well: to equip people, serve them, and provide the resources needed for those you lead. Support looks different for different people, but at its purest form it means to equip and resource them for the journey ahead.

Challenge, on the other hand, means to motivate people by holding them accountable to what they could do if they had the resources. Challenge is the push needed to get people to move to be the best they can be, either as a team or as an individual. For instance, challenge can be direct with words or indirect with action, but the overall purpose of challenge is to help get people to levels that they never imagined they could get to.

How about you? Which do you find more natural, support or challenge, and which one have you had to learn? Which one would those you lead (whether at work or at home) say that you tend to do more?

The 100X-leader journey starts at base camp, where you must understand what your tendencies of support and challenge are by being honest with yourself. This is the first step to getting to 100% health in the way you lead. If you tend to provide high challenge but little support, then own it. Or if you naturally give high support with low challenge, then own that. This is the stage of conscious incompetence (realizing exactly where you are coming up short) and the key to becoming someone people want to follow, rather than have to follow.

Start with Support

To become a person worth following it is vital that you first establish support with those you lead before you challenge them. Starting with support allows for trust to be established relationally so that challenge can be more easily accepted.

John was a vocal leader who expected a lot from his people, and everyone knew it. As general manager, he shared his challenge openly and often. "You know what needs to happen," he would say. "We are down 4% and the big boss won't put up with it. Let's get going!" He would continue to cajole people to execute and "make it happen," on a daily basis.

He was actually quite good at motivating people, and most of the employees did what he asked so they wouldn't get on his "bad side." However, over time John's expectations became unrealistic while the fear of disappointing him or the "big boss" lessened. Although John could overly challenge, his support was earned simply through driving results. In time, the people began to wonder if John truly cared for them or their success. This is where the grumbling and complaining began—to anyone but John.

His team would ask for help on some equipment innovations of this manufacturing company to no avail. "You guys always want something, don't you?" John would say. "No more excuses, let's go. Make it happen." Although they asked for a specific type of machinery to do what he needed them to do, John didn't listen. Over time his team would avoid going to John directly to ask him for anything, because they were always told, "that is what we pay you for—figure it out!"

The harsh challenges to his team became even less effective, and his people did just enough to keep their jobs, but little more. The "big boss" grew more and more frustrated, but because John's team didn't receive the resources they needed, they struggled to hit their quotas.

John became more and more agitated. He eventually went "nuclear" with the ultimate threat of layoffs. His challenge became more and more blatant and threatening as he started to say things like, "Maybe I should just clean house, the whole lot—just start over." He made some layoffs: "That will scare 'em," thought John. However, it only made things worse.

The employees and his team, desperate to save their jobs, started to protect each other against John and the "big boss." Eventually, the employees had enough and began to leave for lateral jobs where they had a better boss. This exodus of employees, coupled with the continued layoffs, turned the culture of the company toxic as the employees told all those looking for employment there to stay away.

The "big boss" started to consider moving the manufacturing plant because, according to John, the workers in this city were "scarce, lazy, and spoiled." Eventually, the company was sold to another private equity group who had more specialism in handling companies that need to be turned around in this sector.

In came the new management team with a similar message: "We know how to turn companies like this around. If you want to keep your jobs then you need to keep your head down, work hard, and do what your leaders say." One midmanager from the manufacturing floor was sent in to ask management for the new equipment to enable them to work smarter. He was quickly told to return to the floor, with the usual response, "That is why we pay you; figure it out."

Unfortunately, there was not a happy ending to this story. The long-term overchallenge and lack of support created a culture rift that affected their market share and their reputation.

If you want to create success with your people or your organization then you must calibrate support before challenge.

> *If you want to create success with your people or your organization then you must calibrate support before challenge.*

The art of leadership, then, is the appropriate calibration of support and challenge at a specific moment, in a specific context for a specific person. When you are trying to establish healthy communication and relational trust it always requires the investment of time. From this perspective support is not soft, it's a strategic decision a leader makes because they understand the long-term return on their investment.

The Support-Challenge Matrix

Years ago, we started to unpack the 100X concepts of support and challenge that was written about in my (Jeremie's) first book, *Making Your Leadership Come Alive (Leadership is Dead)*. We were playing with the liberating/dominating constructs of the book when Steve added two other components, protecting and abdicating, around the four-box matrix he had seen from some work from his friends at DDA Consulting. We then devised a more helpful version of the Support-Challenge Matrix to create a scalable visual tool.

The matrix is simple, but powerful (see Figure 3.1). There are two axes. The y (vertical) axis is support, with high support at the top and low support at the bottom. The x (horizontal) axis is the challenge axis, with low challenge on the left and high challenge on the right. We then created a standard of leadership behavior and the culture that leadership behavior creates in each quadrant.

The best leaders in the world operate in the top right quadrant—they liberate. These leaders have learned how to function by liberating more often each day in every part of their lives and thus have earned the distinction of becoming people worth following.

It is important for you to understand that most of us will visit each quadrant on most days. None of us are perfect. However, the more time we spend in the top right quadrant, the more effective we become. But it doesn't come

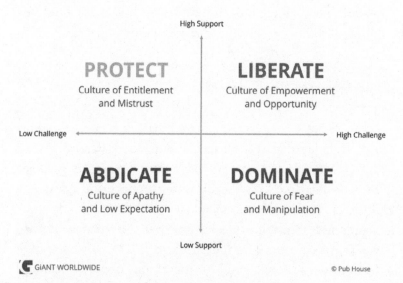

Figure 3.1   The Support-Challenge Matrix
Source: © Support-Challenge Matrix, Pub House/GiANT Worldwide.

naturally! Here is how Nick Green, a British executive of a major corporation, reacted:

> I have been somewhat aware of the fact that I dominate in some situations and abdicate in others, but I've not had the tools to understand what's going on. I was a protector, abdicator, dominator and sometimes liberator—but always subconsciously and never intentionally.
>
> For me the Support-Challenge Matrix was like having cataracts in my eyes fixed. Finally, I could see what was going on and I understood what I was doing and the impact I was having on other people. Initially I applied this new found learning to myself at work, which helped enormously; I realized I could challenge people without it being confrontational!
>
> Then once I'd cracked that and started to do more things intentionally each day, I turned my thoughts to all the other versions of me: the husband, dad, mate in the pub and bloke on the committee.
>
> Seeing my life through the lens of the Support-Challenge Matrix has helped me—and those around me—hugely. I still have to think about what I'm doing—but at least I'm thinking now!

That is our hope for you—we hope you begin to intentionally think about who you are and how you are leading others and in doing so that you might experiencing the fulfillment of being the leader that you have always wanted to be.

Let's look at each of the four quadrants.

Dominating

Very few people choose to dominate other people. It is usually not a conscious decision, and yet most of us have times when we do. Dominating others means that our tendency is to bring challenge, but little support. It is the act of requiring much, but resourcing little, which is not fair to those we lead or love. This often occurs out of habit from stress rather than a deliberate decision.

The dominating quadrant is red, as those who dominate tend to coerce and brow beat people with fear and manipulation when they feel like they aren't winning or if control is slipping out of their grasp. They usually assume that others like them but may be out of touch with the hard reality of what it is like on the other side of themselves as leaders.

Those who have a tendency to dominate are not evil people, of course, but simply focused on getting results by using methods of challenge that bring fear, not empowerment. They don't tend to realize that they are significantly limiting their influence to those they lead because of these actions. We often hear, "But don't you think that there are times when you need to dominate inside the organization?" Our quick reply is, "You mean, do we think there are times when you need to cause fear and manipulation? No, not at all!" There are times when we need to bring more challenge, for sure, but not to abuse power with overcontrol and cause fear or anxiety.

High challenge is only effective if it is calibrated with high support. It must be intentional and thought through. If you react in the moment out of frustration you will normally get it wrong.

Oftentimes, domination comes as a habit, learned from an overbearing parent or coach or boss who yelled in order to get their way. This is simply repeating what you have seen others do around you. Our goal is to get you to the place where you can see what it is like to be on the other side of you and begin to adjust.

Do those who dominate get things done? Absolutely, but so do those who liberate, and the experience of people on the other side of each is dramatically different. Dominating leads to compliance, whereas liberating produces engagement. That difference is what makes leaders great. It is simply not possible to thrive in your work when you are placed in a red culture of fear and manipulation. People eventually burn out and have to be replaced. This is no way to build effective leaders.

Dominating leads to compliance, whereas liberating produces engagement.

Listen to Mike Oechsner, VP of TEAMTRI describe his journey to liberation:

> I realize now that, especially in times of stress, I was a very dominating leader to my team, which, in times of high pressure, already had more than enough challenge facing them. Me bringing more challenge—really, bringing anything other than unqualified support at those times—just magnified the stress, and the challenge I was bringing was unnecessary and unhelpful.
>
> I wasn't taking time to reflect on my lack of influence because I was so busy doing the work and expected everyone else to do what needed to happen when it needed to happen without thinking about getting them engaged instead of having them comply. I look back through texts and e-mails and can see my challenge in my tone and my lack of tact. I am changing and I can see it, but it takes a conscious effort to say the least.
>
> The connection I have with my team gets better, measurably, every day, and in every interaction I'm able to use the Support-Challenge Matrix as a lens. I find myself having fewer conversations about what I could have done better

and having more conversations in the moment asking how I can bring support for great results in communicating, leading, running our events, etc.

When I would dominate, I definitely could get results, but they were at a cost in relationship, influence and rapport. People just didn't want to follow me as much as they had to follow me. That is changing on this journey to liberation and while I am still getting results, the cost is much lower and the rewards are almost immeasurable.

Reflection Questions

1. Who or when do you tend to dominate?
2. What are your typical actions if you tend to give more challenge than support?
3. Do you see people shutting down because of your overchallenge?

Protecting

Those who protect give more support and rarely take time to share challenge or even reasonable expectations. Although this can feel comfortable and easy, ultimately overprotection creates a culture of entitlement and mistrust, as those who protect can flip from Dr. Jekyll to Mr. Hyde in their inconsistent leadership style.

At their core, a person who protects sees even healthy challenge as conflict, and does anything to avoid it, wanting everything to just run smoothly. When there is a need for correction or challenge (or even just setting reasonable expectations), those who protect will tend to hint over and over until they get what they want. "Hey Amy, how are you? Are we all set with the big event next week?" (hint, hint). When they are not satisfied with the results or answer, they come back days later with another hint—"So, Amy, after talking with Brenda I wanted to check back in with you on the event. Are we all set? Is there anything we are missing?" Hinting can be confusing for everyone. One week later and still not happy, the protecting leader can suddenly become quite stern and switch to challenge-only micromanagement. "Amy, this is the third time we have talked about this. I am going to ask Brenda to jump in and help you since she kind of knows what we are working on and you guys will get along great."

All Amy heard was two niceties about the event and then after the third conversation she is now being subverted and replaced by Brenda. Without having a clue why this happened, Amy begins to ask around if anyone else saw this happening. Protecting leaders create sideways energy because they are not clear enough in the beginning with their expectations.

The color of protecting is yellow because these people create caution in their cultures due to the inconsistencies that tend to occur in their leadership style.

Here is an example of a CEO in Atlanta, Georgia, reaching the reality that she was protecting her employees and the effect it had:

Before I'd been introduced to GiANT, I thought I was a personality profile/HR expert and I had nothing to learn. Well, boy, was I wrong! I own a recruiting firm where my employees are part-time moms. With my personality, my natural tendency is to dominate. But I realized during my time with GiANT that I actually protect my staff. I have been overcompensating because I am sympathetic to the life of a stay at home mom/employee. I know that it is hard to do both—so instead of holding to high challenge as would be natural for my personality type—I actually went the other way and gave high support (which I have learned from my 30 years of HR training) and *no* challenge. In fact, I would say, "Oh I understand that you didn't hit your numbers," "Oh, no problem you can't be at our team meeting," etc. But ultimately, the reason I was unhappy with the company was because I felt like I was the only one doing anything.

This January I did a restart of our culture and let all of my staff know that it was a new day, that although I understood their time pressures, we are a business and I'm not responsible for their personal issues. I reminded them that they have a job description and will be held accountable to that. So, I am working toward Liberating where my high support is also met with some high challenge, and I am finding that people are responding very favorably.

—Cindi Filer, CEO Innovative Outsourcing

Whether you lead a business, a nonprofit, or a family, it is important to realize that the best leaders in the world share expectations well, while continuing to give the support that others need.

Reflection Questions

1. Where do you normally hint instead of sharing expectations consistently?
2. Why are you afraid of sharing expectations? What are you afraid of losing with that person?
3. Are you willing to change your style and begin to share your expectations with other people more consistently?

Abdicating

To abdicate means to give up, avoid, relinquish, forgo, abandon, turn one's back on. Abdication usually occurs when people don't fully perform their duties or the responsibilities needed of their role. When a leader abdicates, it can be for many reasons. The leader may be worn out by the overwhelming tasks of the job or have switched off due to office politics or through sheer boredom with lack of challenge. Sometimes, abdication can occur from self-preservation or the fear of being rejected. Whatever the reasons, abdication is a sad place to live or lead. The color for abdication is gray because it creates lifeless cultures with low expectations for all those they lead.

Some people abdicate because they don't believe they have the positional power to shape the culture. This professor shares her reality here:

> You don't need to be the boss to bring meaningful leadership to an organization. I am currently an Associate Professor without a formal leadership position at a public University. Spending 10+ years in academia led me to believe that culture is ingrained and resistant to change, and that it would take more than an inspiring boss to shift ways of thinking. After working with my GiANT Sherpa, I now realize that I was primarily abdicating. Since I was not in a formal leadership position, I thought that it was inappropriate to bring challenge to others. As a team member, I accepted that things happened that were not in my control, and as a result, that passive acceptance made me a likeable and good employee. I did not realize that bringing challenge does not have to be adversarial and can be liberating.
>
> I took the initiative to create an informal support group for junior faculty called "Connected Colleagues."

We meet monthly via videoconference and by utilizing the 100X tools, I have informally coached and mentored my colleagues through difficult discussions, tenure/promotion struggles and helped them recruit new faculty members. My peers now think of me as an influential leader of the faculty and will often seek my opinion before having "tough conversations" with administration or students. This role has given me a tremendous amount of job satisfaction—my colleagues see that my own efficacy has improved as I've learned to lead myself, and they too can benefit from what I've discovered.

—Mary Onysko, Clinical Associate Professor of Pharmacy Practice, University of Wyoming

Reflection Questions

1. Are you burned out or worn out by life or work at this stage?
2. Where are the areas in your life that you are abdicating, and are you ready to reengage?
3. What would need to happen for you to stop abdicating?

Liberating

To liberate is to empower those you lead. We believe that 100X leaders are the best leaders in the world because they have learned how to liberate those they lead in every circle of influence [self, family, team, organization, and community]. The problem is that there are just too few of them in the world. Hopefully, you have experienced someone who has liberated you in your life—maybe a sports coach who was so encouraging that they pushed you to your personal best, or a teacher who gave much of his or her time to get the most out of you. It could have been a parent, a grandparent, or your boss.

One of our friends, Kevin Weaver, wrote a book called *Re-Orient* that shaped our view of the liberating leader concept when he shared this definition—"Love means to fight for the highest possible good in the lives of those you lead . . . until it is a current reality." We have taken that definition as the action of those who liberate; to liberate means to fight for the highest possible good of those you lead.

> *To liberate means to fight for the highest possible good of those you lead.*

Liberating leaders turn things green; they build healthy teams and cultures, and they produce a level of relational trust that takes performance to higher levels. Here is a good example of liberation in action:

I realize now that I had a tendency to dominate inside my organization. Now I have learned how to liberate and I have seen tangible breakthroughs that I would love to share.

I realized that I am responsible for my own leadership journey. As a 100X leader, I am now committed to making sure that I am one of the healthiest people in the room, and constantly look for opportunities to offer support to others in the organization. I also understand the importance of asking for support when needed. I have also become more receptive to external challenge and have learned to approach this with a "nothing is impossible" mindset. The benefits of liberating are numerous. I have developed better relationships with colleagues, there is a greater commitment to accomplishing college initiatives, communication is more transparent, and trust is more evident between us because of the calibration of support and challenge and the consistency that is happening. As someone who now liberates, I appreciate the contributions of others and I know that I am empowered to create opportunities that will positively impact the organization's pursuit towards excellence. Simply stated, I am a much better leader!

—Damita Kaloostian, Dean, South Mountain Community College, Phoenix, Arizona

---

Reflection Questions

1. In what situations do you find it easy to liberate?
2. In what situations do you find it hard to liberate yourself or others?
3. What could you do to improve your liberation of others?

Support Challenge Test

Several years ago, we were helping a manager of a company work through their team culture and specifically his style of leadership. As the Support-Challenge Matrix was drawn on a white board in front of his team, we asked this leader if it was okay to take the support challenge test by getting the team to plot his reality on the matrix. He agreed, but I could tell that his team was nervous about plotting their leader in front of him. I asked the leader to step out of the room and then, one by one, his people came to plot him on the board.

The results were not as the leader expected—the average plot put him square in the dominating category.

As he returned, he tried to make a joke of it, saying, "Come on guys, really? You threw me under the bus in front of him?" When I asked this leader where he would plot himself, he said, "right in the middle" of the liberate quadrant.

The journey from dominating to liberating would be his 100X journey. During the break he confided that he didn't understand it but he wanted to improve, which is the best response when people realize they are consciously incompetent. All leaders with a default tendency toward dominating want to win and want to become more competent. They may just need to be helped to see this reality.

His question was, "How do I bring more support when I thought I already was bringing support?" The answer was, "Ask your team." We then took the next 30 minutes to ask his team what support would look like for them. Here are their surprising answers:

- "It would be nice if you could say hi to us in the morning instead of asking for something from the day before."
- "You are so intense at times that it feels like I have done something wrong. I don't know if you are truly for me."
- "I am thinking about things too, but at times it feels like you don't listen to my ideas and so I kind of just shut down."
- "Ask me how my weekend was."

These are not massive issues, or even difficult things to do, but they all add up to big things long term. Most leaders arrive before their people and have already begun thinking about their days. Oftentimes the leader will begin peppering people about situations or barking orders before their teammates are warmed up. Just remember, little things add up to become big things in the long term, and ultimately your reputation is based on how you make people feel.

A few years later we had another session with this leader and his team. When we did the same exercise, they let us know that he had made it across the liberate line, which quickly led to a smile and a "high-five."

This leader decided to go on the extremely difficult journey of becoming a liberating leader. He has been climbing the mountain, learning tools along the way to become a leader worth following, not just someone that people have to work for. He has been transitioning from a dominating tendency to liberating, both at work and at home.

Your Intent

People are smart. They can smell the leader's intent from a mile away. They tend to know if the leader is for them, for themselves, or against their teams or people.

Are you for people or for yourself?

Most people are not necessarily bad people, they are just living accidental lives and not realizing that they are living incongruently with who they truly want to be. It can be different! Change can happen if you want to become someone worth following.

The questions you need to ask yourself are:

1. Am I truly for my people, or am I for myself?
2. Do they know it? If so, how do they know it?
3. If not, what am I going to do about it?

A Sherpa liberates others only after they have liberated themselves. They then focus on helping others get to the higher levels that they have experienced. When they do, their influence and reputation grows with them.

Note

1. Ronald A. Heifetz, Alexander Grashow, and Marty Linsky,. *The Practice of Adaptive Leadership: Tools and Tactics for Changing Your Organization and the World* (Harvard Business Review Press, 2009).

4

Know Yourself to Lead Yourself

It is not the mountain we conquer but ourselves.
—Edmund Hillary, Mount Everest pioneer

What is true with climbing is true with leadership and life—the higher you climb the harder it gets and the more you must understand yourself. The acclimation to higher levels forces all of us to have to conquer things in our lives that keep us from becoming the person we really want to be. This process takes time and energy, which is why most of us don't do it.

Socrates once said, "The unexamined life is not worth living."

By that, he meant that a lack of intentional growth, reflection, and self-improvement leads to an "accidental life," one in which we settle for lesser versions of our best selves because we fail to put in the time and focus to mold our character and our life into the best it can be.

Equally, one could say that the unexamined leader is not worth following.

In other words, leaders who fail to regularly and intentionally take time to better understand themselves are not the leaders who will bring out the best in themselves or their teams. After all, if we don't know our own strengths, weaknesses, and tendencies under pressure while at work when interacting with others, how can we expect to avoid the pitfalls that sabotage our relational and leadership efforts?

It is now time for you to move toward becoming 100% healthy as a leader. We want you to climb higher—to experience more for your sake and for the sake of everyone who experiences your leadership. We want you to look deeply into your tendencies and make changes. We need more leaders who liberate as a lifestyle. And we hope that you will become a Sherpa to others in the process.

The Other Side of You

Every day you wake up with much on your mind. You go through the daily routines, from hygiene to personal duties to work details. As you walk past people in the halls (or start to interact online), you are plunged into communicating and navigating the mine fields of details, all fraught with problems and drama, and all the while, you may be completely unaware of what it is like to be on the other side of you.

What if we had you followed for a day? What if we had drone or camera footage on your every encounter from the way you treated someone's assistant to the communication at the drive-through to the way you talked with your family. Would you be surprised or even appalled? What would your mother or a special loved one say? What about your kids or key friends—what would they see?

Because most leaders are accidental, they tend to be unaware of the body language shown or the tone and the tact (or lack of it!) that they use or the amount of eye contact they give. These people wonder why others respond the way they do.

Years ago, we were doing some leader interviews with senior leaders of a large global company. One of their leaders, a competent individual performer, had challenges with his leadership, as everyone was afraid of him. When we first met with him, he had his arms crossed and a furrowed brow on his face and sternly asked us, "How long is this going to take?"

Our questions were centered on his awareness of his body language, but we could tell he wasn't getting it. Our question was direct—"Why are you so angry?" His response as he sat with angry eyes and crossed arms was classic, "I am not, I have never been happier. Seriously, I am having such a great season." We laughed and joked if we could take a picture to show him what it was like to be on the other side of him.

This leader simply didn't understand what most don't—in extreme busyness leaders lose influence, which keeps people from wanting to follow them. Are you wondering why you were passed over for that last promotion? It may be the lack of self-awareness.

> *In extreme busyness leaders lose influence, which keeps people from wanting to follow them.*

At minimal levels of self-awareness and emotional intelligence, it is impossible for leaders to climb very high; they are just not acclimated to the culture or climate around them, even though it may be obvious to everyone else. Without acclimation in self-awareness it is impossible for you to lead others up to the next level in the same way that it is impossible

You can't lead people where you haven't been yourself.

for you to go to these levels yourself. You can't lead people where you haven't been yourself.

The Journey of Self-Awareness

The most important part of any leadership journey is the ongoing, never-ending process of self-awareness. For all the many books, articles, and experts who talk about it, self-awareness can be boiled down to two simple commitments:

1. A commitment to understand how you're wired, the tendencies that result from such wiring, and the impact those tendencies have on others.
2. A commitment to change your negative tendencies in order to become the best person and leader you can be.

One of the most potent tools we created to train 100X leaders is called Know Yourself to Lead Yourself. The infinity symbol in Figure 4.1 represents the need for constant, continuous reflection on the components of behavior and consequence that shape our reality as our influence.

If we start at the bottom of the diagram and work our way around it counterclockwise, we discover the process of how our actions and tendencies shape us.

Tendencies

We all have tendencies that create patterns of actions and behavior that generate consequences that ultimately shape our current reality. Therefore, if we want to change our reality—if

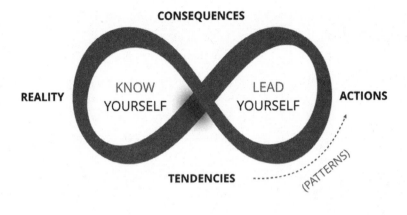

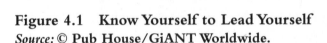

Figure 4.1 Know Yourself to Lead Yourself
Source: © Pub House/GiANT Worldwide.

our marriage is struggling or our team is underperforming—
we must find the tendencies that form the patterns of action,
which are generating the undesired consequences. Only by
understanding the connection between these elements can
we intentionally and accurately target the areas of growth and
learning that will bring about the reality we desire for ourselves as well as those we love and lead.

Our tendencies will never change—they are hard wired
into our DNA and our personality. This is what we call our
Nature, which is the hand you have been dealt. It is therefore
vital to catalogue our tendencies as our tendencies so we can
know ourselves and lead ourselves.

- What do you tend to do when you are angry?
- What is your tendency when you have not received the
  honor you think you deserve?

- How do you handle incompetence in others?
- How do you feel when you are under stress?
- What do you tend to do when you don't get your way?

This is a start to understanding your tendencies as you become more self-aware. Since tendencies will never change, it is vital to see the patterns that come from your tendencies.

Patterns

Take a moment to think about what you do under pressure. What do you do when you get frustrated? What default patterns do you tend to fall into when you're embarrassed or when you feel like someone is trying to control you?

Now think about the kinds of patterns those repeated reactions begin to create. Since we all have default tendencies, which, if left unattended, become default patterns and actions, the accidental leader is very predictable. You will hear people say, "That's just Sarah, you know what she is like." Or, "You know Tom; he just gets defensive. You have to work around him." The truth is, we are all conditioned to develop certain patterns of action that left alone can do considerable damage and create a reputation that we certainly wouldn't choose to have.

A pattern might look like a slammed door with frustration or a defensive tone when confronted or a glare when spoken down to. A pattern might also look like a person procrastinating because of the tendency to abdicate. A pattern is something you do over and over again thinking it produces results, but it rarely does. People know your patterns, and if you ask them they will tell you.

Patterns can be manifested as an external behavior or as an internal thought and both must be managed in order to become a leader worth following.

Actions

Each action we perform based on our patterns creates a consequence, which is a reaction to our actions. Self-aware people know their tendencies and default patterns of behavior and at times choose an action contrary to the default.

The intentional journey from tendency to action is what defines the leaders who climb the highest. They are able to choose actions that are not their default patterns when they know to do so would be unhelpful. Some leaders are unconsciously incompetent; they don't understand what it's like to be on the other side of them. Others have climbed a little higher and know their tendencies and patterns but still lapse back into becoming unaware where their tendencies become their actions again. Sadly, none of us ever graduate from the school of self-awareness, so every day has to be an intentional choice to know ourselves and lead ourselves accordingly.

> *We never graduate from the school of self-awareness.*

Unaware people, then, cause reactions to their actions all day long because they are unaware that their actions cause consistent drama with those in their lives. This lack of awareness can be quite frustrating as these types of people tend to blame everyone else instead of seeing the obvious acts that caused the entire drama.

Charlie provokes people for amusement. Terry exaggerates every slight. Donna walks away when confronted. John tends to gossip about everything. Dan is late for every meeting without fail. These are the actions of everyday people in our everyday lives—you can change the names, but the actions are the same. The list of actions can go on and on, but the key is for you to think about yourself. What are your consistent actions that you could control if you became more intentional about knowing and leading yourself? Remember, your actions come from your tendencies and patterns, and they lead to consequences that shape your reality. If you want to change your reality, then you must change your patterns and actions.

You can't blame a leader for being unconsciously incompetent. The job of a Sherpa is to hold up a mirror and help leaders become consciously incompetent in order for them to get to the next level. That is what the 100X journey is all about.

Consequences

There is a price tag to our unconsidered patterns and actions: the consequences of our words, deeds, retorts, and responses. They shape who we are, how we think, how we interact, and the way other people learn to view and interact with us as a result.

Consequences are the ramifications of actions—the result of behavior. If you don't like the consequences that you are experiencing, then it is important to look at the actions and work backward to the patterns and tendencies. Most people tend to blame others when the consequences they are experiencing aren't favorable. However, the appropriate response comes in self-awareness and asking yourself what part you played in the consequence. The mature and secure leader will then become responsive and work to make things right, where the immature and insecure leader will simply react to the actions, producing even more negative consequences.

Obviously, consequences are not always bad. A changed pattern can create a positive action, which produces a good consequence rather than a negative one.

Either way, all consequences ultimately shape current reality. So, in light of the consequences, it is vital to be intentional about the patterns we develop so that we produce positive consequences rather than negative.

Reality

Do you like your reality?

Some of you might be experiencing a turf war with another department in a company. That is your reality. Some of you might not be on speaking terms with your adult children. Again, another form of reality, all because of patterns that come from actions.

Reality is the result of our natural tendencies growing into patterns with actions that produced consequences that we now get to live with. Most people complain about their realities without ever acknowledging that their own actions and tendencies are at least partly (or entirely) responsible.

If we are unaware of the subtle tendencies that create our patterns, then we are forfeiting control of our own reality. By remaining unaware of those tendencies, and therefore being unintentional about the patterns we create, we are no longer the masters of our own destinies.

Another way to use the Know Yourself to Lead Yourself tool is to work backward. Pick a reality that you don't like and review it honestly—ask yourself what were the actions that created the mess that you are in. Once you've identified the actions, look at your behavior patterns and observe what your natural tendencies are. Be honest here with yourself or ask a friend to work through it with you.

A wildfire only takes a cigarette flung from a vehicle by a careless, preoccupied person to start an inferno. In the same way, a habitual pattern of an eye roll or a harsh tone or a slammed door can lead to years of dysfunctional relationships.

So far as it depends on each of us, we need to manage ourselves well so that we produce the right outcomes and shape the best realities.

The Biggest Problem in Leadership

The lack of self-awareness is the biggest leadership problem in the world. This issue causes a lack of trust that derails organizations, stymies teams, and causes people to lose sleep because of the crippling stress that comes from unawareness. Most people just don't see that they have broccoli in their teeth, but these same people often love to point out the broccoli they see in others!

Without taking the time to fully identify our tendencies and evaluate negative impact in our lives and on the people around us, we can never truly gain control of our own reality. We lose the ability to change our outcomes and instead, remain captive to our tendencies and the paths they dictate for us.

Fortunately, we have a say in all this. We can choose to become intentional about knowing our own tendencies and commit to changing them. Self-awareness is choosing to commit to diving deep into your own wiring, learning to understand the knee-jerk reactions you have been conditioned to exhibit over the years, and choosing to know yourself so that you can lead yourself in the effort to create the reality you desire.

It's not easy, but it is doable. Use the tool to develop the skill of self-awareness and you will see the fruit of your hard work. The good news is, you don't have to be defined by your tendencies. You have the power to shape your own reality. So, step up, lean into it, and become a master at leading yourself.

The Transformed Leader

Mickey Daniel is one of the most amazing leaders we have ever met. We first met him in Atlanta, Georgia, when he joined a GiANT yearlong leadership journey and the transformation that has taken place over the years since then has been unbelievable.

Mickey is a leader inside Georgia Power and he has also been an accomplished high school football coach over the years. He decided to climb the mountain and along the way he found some hard things about what it was like to be on the other side of him. Here is his story about how he became self-aware and changed his reality:

From looking at the Support-Challenge Matrix, I thought I was dominating in many circles of influence in my life. Though I had left the profession of coaching, my experience as the offensive line coach on staff of one of the all-time winningest coaches in Georgia history had left a lasting impression on my leadership style. For years, I used my position of authority to drive athletes as hard as possible. Winning required sacrifice and I challenged athletes daily to compete to be the best as I *demanded* excellence. Since football in the United States is traditionally a "hard-nosed" sport, no exceptions were allowed—anything less than winning was a failure.

Sadly, my dominating influence didn't stop on the field, it carried over to my family far too frequently. The father of two sons, I wanted them to be the best. They had to outwork everyone and "work before play" was my motto for our family. After nearly destroying my family, I realized it was football or my family—I chose my family and walked away from the sport I loved.

This decision was one of the best decisions of my life. As I proceeded with the journey, I asked my family to plot me on the Support-Challenge Matrix. My youngest son was clearly nervous, and I asked him, "Are you afraid to take this because I am a Dominator to you?" to which he responded with an emotional, "Yes." My heart broke as I realized that it was going to take a lot to mend what I had blown up. The same was true with my wife—those I cared the most about received the full brunt of my challenge with no support. Not only did they not feel like I was for them, but at times, they even felt like I was against them!

The GiANT team taught me that I could still deliver challenge, but I could be a much more effective leader by ensuring I balanced it with support. Though I'm not perfect, I am a work in progress who is now aware of my tendencies, and I strive to be a great leader of my family and my team.

My relationships with my wife, my sons, and those I lead are at an entirely different level. We've all been liberated. I simply became self-aware and began to change my patterns and actions. My goal now is to take others up the mountain as well, which is exactly the point of 100X, of being a Sherpa as you liberate others.

Why You Must Go First

"I really want my people to get your principles because they need to hear this," is a phrase we often hear after speaking to audiences full of leaders. Our usual response is, "You need to live out the principles yourself first!"

Most leaders think they are good but believe that their people have issues. This is not totally true. Your "people" are an indication of you. The leader defines the culture. If you have influence and are in charge of a large group of people and have been there for some length of time, then you are responsible for leading them, taking them up the mountain, while supporting and challenging them to become the team they need to be. If that is not happening, then we must go back to you—*it starts with you.*

It is impossible to train others to be something that they don't see in you. However, when your people see in you what they want to be, you are on the right track. When your people see you doing the hard jobs, over communicating for clarity, challenging others, and supporting them at the same time, then you will have the influence to help others change.

Leadership is about you knowing yourself, addressing the issues, and leading yourself to healthy outcomes. When people see you do it first, they tend to imitate what they see. When you are leading well, generally people will follow.

So, as you work your way through the 100X tools contained in this book, apply it to yourself first, and show the change in yourself that you want to see in others. When they see you do it they will be more apt to do it themselves. It is a simple concept, but hard to do, and rarely gets implemented.

Who Would You Follow?

Who are the people in your life that are truly worth following? What do you notice about the way they live and lead? Have you observed how much they lead themselves?

The leaders that we know who are worth following are focused on becoming 100% healthy; they know their tendencies and own them, and they work hard to improve their patterns for the good of everyone.

This is why the Sherpa analogy works so well. After talking with climbers in the Himalayas and reading countless stories about the Sherpa, they truly are worth following up a mountain as their focus is consistently to help others climb. Helping others see their unconscious incompetence and leading them gently to a new level of self-awareness and health is what the best leaders in the world do.

Healthy leaders who have earned the right because of their own self-awareness to intentionally transfer their learning to others have become leaders that others will choose to follow. Now, let's take a look at how aware you are in every circle of influence.

5 | Five Circles of Influence

*The way to liberation is to allow the invasiveness
of the journey or process. To become a leader worth
following you must focus on every area of your life
and that is usually the most difficult thing to do.
Becoming a person worthy of following means that
you must look inward into the mirror and make significant changes in areas that you didn't think you
would need to. It is a hard journey, which is why so
many leaders stay at the lower levels.*
—Pattye Moore, Chairman of the Board, Red
Robin Gourmet Burgers and former President,
Sonic

To become a 100X leader—a person worth following—you must change the patterns that come from your default tendencies as you acclimate to higher levels of leading and change your patterns of abdication, domination, or protection to move to liberation. This must occur in every circle of life, not just at work.

If you want to go high, you must first go deep.

Geologically, the depth of the valley defines the height of the mountain. If you want to go high, you must first go deep.

Five Circles of Influence

When most people think about getting better at leading people they normally think about leading people at work. And yet, we have found that if you don't include self-leadership or family leadership then you will never truly fulfill your true potential or function at the higher levels of influence.

In the Industrial Age, before the digital revolution, the mindset of the leader was far more compartmentalized than it is today. What you did at home didn't affect your ability to lead at work. In the digital world that is not the same, since social media and technology have encroached into every area of our lives. People are now looking for leaders who are authentic and genuinely model integrity and consistency in every area. It is almost impossible not to remain connected to the world at large all day, multitasking while seeing news of an old college friend or receiving texts from your spouse or kids while working. This connectedness forces us to be nimble as we are constantly dealing with issues in all the five circles of influence: self, family, team, organization, and community. Figure 5.1 shows a simple, but powerful tool we use to liberate others.

INTENTIONAL

COMMUNITY

ORGANIZATION

TEAM

FAMILY

SELF

ACCIDENTAL

GIANT WORLDWIDE

© Pub House

Figure 5.1 The Five Circles of Influence
Source: © **Pub House/GiANT Worldwide.**

Influence is an inside-out game. You must look inward before leading outward. This issue is precisely why we have so many ineffective leaders in the world. They are trying to lead from the team and organization circles but are woefully inept when it comes to leading at the self and family circles. The unaware leader doesn't understand that they need to address these areas if they want to be an authentic 100X leader in this age.

We constantly deal with leaders who are achievers and are most driven to excel at work. It is in the team or organization circle where they also receive most of their rewards, so they tend to stay focused on these circles of influence instead of the more personal areas. However, if the self and family circles are ignored, the tendency to become unstable in crisis goes up dramatically. They are seen as less than authentic leaders. The key is to focus on all five circles of influence.

Intentional versus Accidental

On a mountain, everything must be intentional. Life depends on it. The Sherpa are constantly thinking ahead, observing those they are leading up the mountain and understanding their own strength in order to succeed and keep everyone safe along the way. This is intentional leadership.

Accidental living is living by chance, unintentionally. It is hoping for things just to work out but not doing anything to make it occur. Accidental leadership is similar. "We hope people just do their job, that's why we hired them, right?" This laissez-faire approach to life is easier in the front end but has potentially dangerous consequences. Intentional living and leading are much harder up front but will produce much better outcomes in the long run.

Therefore, the journey toward liberating leadership begins with intentionality. It's rooted in a willingness to look in the mirror, or even let others hold up a mirror for you to see what it's like to be on the other side of you. What is it like to be led by you? Loved by you? Live with you? What tendencies do you have that build others up or bring them down, and are those tendencies increasing or decreasing your influence with them?

The Path to Liberating Leadership This sort of self-honesty is a challenge for everyone. It requires being secure in who you are and having the humility to commit to a process of uncovering your weaknesses. Our natural tendencies don't really change but with intentionality, humility, and effort we can begin to have a choice between the default patterns of how we normally respond to a situation and what we actively choose to do or say instead.

The best leaders are intentional about this process and invite others to help them see where they can improve. Our best description of the leaders who commit to this challenge, came from our friend Pat Lencioni, when he shared that they are humble, hungry, and smart.[1] Humble enough to admit, "I really want to grow, and invite others to help me"; hungry because they decided, "I really don't want to stay the way I am"; and smart enough to be able to learn and commit to that learning and growth over a period of time.

Intentionality Leads to Consistency Intentional leadership is not for the faint of heart. After all, accidental leadership is the definition of default mode. It's easy, it's reactionary, and it doesn't require facing our weaknesses or embracing our learning opportunities. And it certainly doesn't require inviting others to challenge us in that process.

The truth is, most leadership fails because the leader is inconsistent or accidental, succumbing too easily to the whims of self-preservation and knee-jerk reactions. It would be like an accidental Sherpa on Mount Everest. Can you even imagine? Would anyone want to follow them up the mountain when they are responsible for placing ladders over crevasses or ropes up steep cliffs? No, we only want to follow an intentional and consistent Sherpa.

When you become consistent, you display your health, both as a leader and a person. And when you become healthy, your influence grows dramatically. Then, you start winning because your influence wins. Your team starts winning as well as you grow to become a more cohesive team. You start feeling at peace with yourself and begin to trust one another. With that security comes confidence and humility, which makes people begin to respect you even more.

That's what it means to liberate and be liberated.

The Self Circle

Let's start with the first circle of Self and then work our way out as we attempt to mash up the Support-Challenge Matrix (from Chapter 2) with the Five Circles of Influence and ask yourself the following: Who are you to yourself? Do you dominate yourself? Do you protect or abdicate? Or do you tend to liberate yourself?

All of us have an inner voice. Some of us speak positively about ourselves, while many speak horrible things about themselves: "You really have no idea what you're talking about." "No one wants to listen to you." "You're not a very good parent." "You are never going to get fit, you just don't have what it takes."

As we wrote this book, we studied in depth the mental preparation of extreme climbers and the Sherpa in particular. It was clear that the Sherpa view climbing differently than their clients, who see climbing as something to check off their bucket list. The Sherpa conversely are climbing in reverence of the living Mount Everest, which they call *Chomolungma,* which means "mother of the world," while working to keep those they lead healthy and safe. To do this well, the Sherpa must think positively about themselves and eliminate any negatives. Here is what a few Sherpa shared about leading themselves in their interview with researcher, Kate O'Keefe:[2]

- "We always think positive, there are no negative things…" (Sherpa 1).
- "… whenever we start an expedition … we think that we are going to be successful" (Sherpa 5).

- "...but we think when we start that we will be definitely going to the summit...we have good hope and we think we will be a success" (Sherpa 2).
- "we wish and we will try to do our best and summit mostly all climbers...Yeah we think first, that we will do it" (Sherpa 3).

For some of you, overcoming the negative is the biggest barrier to climbing the mountain. You must liberate yourself. No more domination! No more overchallenge and under-support. What would it look like if you spoke positively about yourself by showing yourself grace while still being accountable to being the best you can be?

For some of you it is time to increase the challenge as you have been giving yourself too much support. "Oh, it's okay, you deserve it; you have been working so hard," as you allow yourself to indulge in one more of this or that. It is such a fine line when it comes to our mental makeup, as our personality, past experiences, beliefs, and influences of others shape much of our mental makeup. Some people have given up, whereas some give themselves too much slack, and others are taskmasters to themselves.

To liberate is to give freedom. Our minds produce the actions that come from our hearts. Therefore, as people trying to be helpful or successful we must start the inside journey first in the way we treat and think about ourselves. This is in no way selfish, but it rather bolsters the simple idea—you can't give what you don't possess. If you want to help others you must be healthy first. The airlines demonstrate this well before every flight: "In the event of an emergency place the oxygen mask on yourself first before helping the person next to you." Why? Because if you are not breathing you can't help others breathe.

Reflection Exercise

Take a few minutes and ask yourself the following
questions before moving on to the next sections of this
chapter:

1. How do you treat yourself, at different times? When
   do you liberate, dominate, protect, or abdicate?
2. As it relates to the self circle, are you generally intentional or accidental?
3. What needs to change as it relates to leading yourself?

The Family Circle

Family, in whatever form that is to you, is vital in all our lives.
The reason it is so important is that those closest to us can
either help us become more effective or they can distract us
from becoming our best.

   Family can be a blessing to the soul or, at worst, a thorn
in the side—usually due to neglect or abdication or historical
issues. Some leaders spend all their time and attention on other
parts of their lives (often team or organization), assuming that
family is the spouse's responsibility. If the family is ignored,
however, because of accidental living, the ramifications will
be unfortunate and long term. This leader, who asked to be
anonymous shares his reality here:

   I don't know what to say. I am torn. My desire is to liberate my family, but I am constantly dealing with a situation
   where I don't feel alive at home. I think my years of abdicating at home has created lower expectations of my wife
   and myself to our future together. I have been accidental
   and I know it and now I am suffering the consequences and

I don't know what to do. Therefore, I tend to dominate at times, protect at other times, and end up abdicating. I don't know how to liberate at this point in our marriage.

In the family circle, an experienced Sherpa is intentional. She or he uses support and challenge consistently, usually in different ways than they might at work. Here is how one client brought the process of liberation to her family:

In my parenting I realized I swing from Protecting to Dominating in the way I lead my kids. In an effort to make my 16-year-old behave and perform at a top level I realized I am probably giving too much challenge and sharing high expectations in my tone with too little support. In fact, I don't know exactly how to support him. I am using the Support-Challenge Matrix to help me learn how to help get my son to the next level.

—Molly Holm, Owner and Chief Creative Officer at Glory

Some of us might tend to dominate our spouses or children, and others may tend to protect family or close friends. Whichever it is, we all have patterns, and if we understand them, we can begin to alter them positively. In much of our work with highly driven, ambitious leaders, we find that abdication is the norm when it comes to families. What would happen for your family if you chose to liberate them, to calibrate high support as you fight for their highest possible good? What would help them? Have you tried asking?

Family can be the most difficult area to liberate because we are dealing with kids of differing ages and maturity levels, and we are often trying to co-parent with someone else who has their own tendencies and patterns. For some, the real issue is that one spouse might not have the positional authority at home as they do at work, where hierarchies are clearer. In contrast, at home it is supposed to be a partnership, but it only works if you take the time to truly understand what it looks like to liberate your spouse.

Scott Cornelius, a husband and dad living in San Francisco, explains his tendency and difficulty in being consistent as a parent:

> I realize now that I was primarily protecting my family. But now I've learned how to liberate and I've seen tangible breakthroughs to celebrate. As parents, we want nothing but success and happiness for our kids. I literally wanted them to experience nothing but rainbows and unicorns. However, through the Support-Challenge Matrix I am reminded of the importance of both rainbows and valleys. It is important for my kids to experience both these honestly and that I don't shelter them from their consequences or criticism. True growth and liberation requires both support and challenge.

That is what a Sherpa does in the family circle. They liberate their children to live through real highs and lows, teaching them how to rise to challenges and move on from failures, while supporting and nurturing them.

Reflection Exercise

1. What is your tendency with each member of your family? Do you treat them differently?
2. What would they say about you? Would you be willing to ask them?

The Team Circle

You may have already thought about your tendencies of support and challenge as they relate to your team because of the previous chapter, but we want you to go deeper. A team could be any group of people working on a common goal. Our goal for you is for you to become consistent in your support and challenge and let's admit it, some team-mates cause us to want to protect or abdicate or dominate. The reality is that a different calibration is required for each person on your team.

People are difficult and so is consistent leadership. Gavin Loftus, an executive living in the UK, says it this way:

> Hindsight is a wonderfully humbling thing. Our business was growing rapidly, with all the challenges that come with it. There was always an issue to address, a problem to solve or a project to deliver and my team was under pressure.
>
> My default position when a problem came up was "Give it here, I'll fix it." Things did get sorted out, but I would spend my days firefighting rather than investing and planning for the future. I thought I was helping my team out. I thought that's what good leaders did.
>
> The Support-Challenge Matrix helped me see that I was protecting my people. I had my team's interests at heart but in shielding them by taking the work myself, I wasn't giving them the opportunity to step up to the challenge. By being a Protector, I was shortsighted, and I paid the cost. It wasn't long until I burnt out.
>
> My GiANT Sherpas helped me to see that a good leader balances support with challenge. I learnt the difference between supporting someone and doing it for him or her! I've found it much easier to bring challenge with this simple tool to work from.

Now, we have more people who can take ownership of projects and overcome challenges themselves. We are able to grow more, and the business is in a much healthier place than it was when I was trying to do everything myself. As I said, hindsight is a wonderfully humbling thing.

Teams must be led by people who can properly support and challenge their people to perform at higher levels.

Reflection Exercise

1. What does your team say about you after the Support-Challenge Matrix exercise?
2. What are your tendencies in the team circle?
3. What kind of leader would you like to be?

The Organization Circle

Paula Tulley is the Regional Commercial and Marketing Lead, PEH Europe at Pfizer. After going through our one-year XCore program she discusses her learning inside her organization:

I realized that inside my organization I was often in the Liberate quadrant, which was comforting to see and yet I also realized that at times I became accidental and started to protect more than liberate.

My breakthrough has been realizing that in tough times, as a leader, I need to communicate my expectations more clearly. These practical tools helped me become much more intentional with my language which helps with my leadership throughout the organization. Inside my organization I strive to be clear but fair ... what more can anyone ask?

Organizations are made up of subcultures—teams with the healthiest subcultures are normally tied to the healthiest organizations. If team leaders are deliberate in the way they lead, then they will receive the results of great teams, healthy groups of people fighting for the highest possible good of one another. Although we talk about this in depth in a later chapter, it is important to understand that the strength of a team—and thus, the organization—lies in the strength of team leaders leading well in their subculture.

Reflection Exercise

1. What is your reputation with regard to your organization?
2. What are your tendencies in the organizations you are involved with?
3. Do you see yourself as a liberator, even in areas that you can't control?

The Community Circle

The community circle consists of community inside neighborhoods, associations, churches, book clubs, and groups of all different shapes and sizes. How you lead in this circle could affect your reputation and influence it in big ways.

My (Jeremie's) community has changed dramatically over the past few years. In a five-year window our community shifted three distinct times—from Atlanta to London to Oklahoma City. With each move, we changed our community. As we moved back to our hometown for our kids' high school we decided to build a community in the form of an actual neighborhood called the Prairie at Post. Although we have been very intentional in our new development, we completely abdicated in our current neighborhood, while we waited for the new. We thought we would only live in this current neighborhood for a year and therefore we didn't build deep roots because of the upcoming move. The issue for my wife and me was that we have been building a liberating community elsewhere, while abdicating in our current location, which is something we are trying to change.

To each of us, community can mean different things. It is important to realize the impact that each of you have or could have within your communities, whether through a nonprofit, neighborhood, or school association or a church or different group.

Reflection Exercise

1. What do you consider to be your community circle?
2. Are you engaged in your community at the right level?
3. Where do you believe you could become more effective in your community?

Support Challenge plus Five Voices Color Code Test

If you take the Support-Challenge Matrix and review it against the Five Circles of Influence, you will have the chance to see a snapshot of your behaviors in each circle of influence in the current moment. The joy of this process is that you can change your behavior almost overnight if you choose to become intentional rather than accidental. This will allow

 GiANT WORLDWIDE   © Pub House

Figure 5.2   Five Circles of Influence
Source: © **Pub House/GiANT Worldwide.**

you to reach the next level, which you may have doubted was possible. It is a process you can repeat regularly.

To go through this exercise, you must honestly assess what your actions tend to be in each circle (see Figure 5.2) and color-code them accordingly. Liberating is green; dominating is red; abdicating is gray; and protecting is yellow. What are you to yourself? Your family? Your team and your organization? What about your community?

When you see what you tend to do in each circle it should or could have a profound effect on the way you support or lead those closest to you. Our goal as your Sherpa is to help you get rid of your incongruence and become more aligned as you live and lead.

Putting It All Together

Diana Bocaneala, Head of People Development and Recruitment at Endava CE in Romania, summarizes the journey of liberation like this:

> I realize now that I was primarily dominating my team, causing things to turn red. When I became aware of this I saw that the environment I created around myself was not one that would sustain my personal growth or that of the team. I decided to strive to liberate the people I lead! As a result, I've seen team members embracing the challenge I bring to them with the confidence that I will be there for them and support them to breakthrough. I've seen good people becoming great, now confident that they can do it too, they can conquer the mountains, and they do.
>
> In my family, though, I was primarily protecting them. I can't express in words how painful this was for me to acknowledge that due to my behavior, I've created a culture of mistrust. For me it was a paradigm change. My husband went through some difficult moments and my attitude had been to protect him, take on the responsibility and overcome the issues by myself, thinking this was a way to show my love. When I realized what I had built and that actually to love and trust means to have the confidence that the one who you've chosen to be with forever has the capability, has the resources and skills to be and do more and better, made me rethink how I address the challenges and share the opportunity to serve and love with him. The last year was like our second honeymoon, after 11 years of marriage, we rediscovered each other.
>
> In my community I was abdicating. For a long time, I was not doing anything for the local community. It was easy to sit and judge that things were not happening the

way they should. I realized that this was not the right attitude and if I wanted to change anything, I should start with myself and change my attitude. So I shared with the local youth group about what I'm doing in my company and offered to help. I started to work with them and help them to be liberating leaders for themselves and for the community they are part of and together, as I'm writing this, we are building a strategy for the community youth and I'm sure that great results will come in the upcoming years.

We have hopefully given you some food for thought. You may even be feeling a little challenged or consciously incompetent in a few areas. Here are some answers to common questions we are asked at this stage, from our Liberator Podcast and during consulting sessions to help you integrate this in to your real life:

What do I do if I dominate people in multiple circles of influence?

In our experience we encounter far more dominating leaders (and therefore dominating cultures) in the business world than in not-for-profits, where leaders are more commonly protecting those they lead. Some of you might be wondering if you do this. Kayla Kersey, Chief Administrative Officer for TLC Plumbing & Utility in New Mexico, will answer what she experienced for herself:

The first time I saw the Support-Challenge Matrix I immediately realized that I am primarily a Dominator in most of my circles of influence. Some, like my immediate team, who I felt truly knew the real me, understood that the high challenge I shared was not only calibrated with some support for them, but also directed mostly internally—at myself.

However, when I shared this same level of expectation with others in my Organization circle that I didn't see or work with every day, it was received as fear-inducing manipulation, as self-promotion and not supportive of the overall empowerment of the organization. In an "aha" moment I realized that I was constantly undermining my influence and creating a culture of fear. I thought I was being helpful by taking some weight off others' shoulders, solving their problems, getting their jobs done, boldly sharing my ideas of how to improve something, and not being afraid to ask the difficult questions or make the difficult decisions. I thought I was bringing value to the Organization and was showing I cared. While all those things I mention ARE of value, I learned that you could be right and wrong at the same time when doing any of them! I have learned to Liberate not by lowering my challenge, but increasing my support. Now I truly allow people in my organization to participate in solving the problems, I let others take the credit for accomplishments, leave room for them to share ideas and I don't jump to the solution first.

What are practical ways I can improve my dominating tendencies?

If you want to improve your patterns and move toward liberating others, here are five practical steps you can take:

1. **Understand the power of your actions.** Show people you are willing to grow by changing your patterns and creating a culture of empowerment and growth.
2. **Learn how to add *support* into your world.** Ask those in your life what support looks like for them so that you can consistently liberate instead of dominate.
3. **Give people the chance to begin their mornings well.** Often, dominating is missing the little things. Practice saying hello and goodbye. Stop the curt responses and try this, "Hey Dan, good morning. How are you?" Most

dominators are afraid that Dan will tell them how he is doing and start a lengthy conversation, when in reality that is a normal morning hello. By taking a few minutes to be courteous, a person with dominating tendencies can watch their influence meters move up drastically compared to what they are currently receiving.

4. **Learn how to challenge more effectively.** There are some gifted challengers we know. The best challengers get the most out of people because others know that they are for them, not against them. Learn from the best and try adding tact and insight. To challenge is both an art and science, because it means you are being intentional in other people's lives for their best interests.

5. **Become more consistent.** It is okay to fight as long as people know that you are willing to serve. You lead people well when you serve and support people and fight for and challenge those you lead consistently for a long period of time.

Yelling, manipulating, and inducing fear never produce the long-term results that leaders desire. They are the actions of a lazy leader who is consumed by their own tasks and only interested in those who can serve them or help them win. If you sow seeds of support into your people along with healthy challenge when needed, you will create a culture that is green both in health and in financial return.

What do I do if I tend to protect people in multiple circles of influence?

This is a natural situation, especially at home. Here are some practical things you can do to move from protecting to liberating.

1. **Evaluate the reality that has occurred because of your protection.** This tends to show up in kids being spoiled because of child-centered parenting. Protecting means to

keep people from growth, because your lack of sharing expectations can rob people of growing in their capacity to handle life. Where then is it happening?

2. **Practice sharing expectations.** We will discuss this later, but sharing what winning looks like or what you want to occur is natural and healthy. Share your appropriate expectations with consistency and watch what liberation can look like.

3. **When you feel like coddling, push through to do the right thing.** It may feel uncomfortable at first, but the long term will be so worth it. Most protecting is simple years of oversupporting and low challenge that finally becomes an issue.

Everyone has something to learn. This long-term client experienced a breakthrough about his reality:

I realized that I was overprotecting my staff after going through the 100X journey. As CEO, I had created a team that would ride through fire by my side but that had become comfortable with the day to day, reducing the chance of growth and opportunity. After practicing bringing more challenge and learning to liberate, I now have staff who believe they can achieve more than ever before. I also have a team who feels that they are fairly treated and do not carry the weight of others. I am still learning how to fight commensurate to the way I serve so that I can become consistent long term with those I lead.

—**Mark Lewington, CEO, CTS Systems**

What if I think I am liberating others but they don't agree?

You have to be authentic in all five circles of influence. What you believe to be liberation might be received as condescension or nagging. You might try explaining the Support-Challenge Matrix, expressing your desire to liberate and then asking the group for some honest feedback. Ask them what it is really like to be on the other side of you (and don't get defensive when they tell you!). Ask them to plot you on the matrix and truly listen to them. Thank them for being honest.

People need to know that you are for them and need to see that you are genuine in your desire to grow personally. This humility in receiving feedback and owning your own weakness is powerful and will encourage others to do the same.

As a Sherpa for you, our greatest desire is that you would become intentional and consistent in your ability to function in 100% health and learn how to liberate others more often each day in each circle of influence. If you do this you will eventually receive the rewards that all leaders value most—honor, respect, and lasting influence.

The 100X journey takes time. Some of you will take much longer on 100% health, while some of you are ready for the X of multiplication. In the next chapter, we will explore how to develop others to get them to the higher levels.

Notes

1. Courtesy of Patrick Lencioni.
2. Kate O'Keefe, "The Mental Strategies of Elite Climbing Sherpa" (Master's thesis, University of Jyväskylä, 2016).

Getting Others to a Higher Level

6 | The Higher Levels

Wise man is a good Sherpa; he takes you
to the highest places!
—Mehmet Murat Ildan

At 29,029 feet (roughly 8,850 meters), climbing Mount Everest is deemed one of the most difficult and dangerous feats on earth.

For most of us, climbing Mount Everest is an unrealistic dream, but the brave few pay the cost, both financially and physically, to attempt the impossible. Out of approximately 5,000 people who have climbed to the top of the world, roughly 300 of those climbers have perished on the mountain since records began.

Climbing Mount Everest is hard enough. Without the Sherpa, reaching the summit would stay a dream to most. It is virtually impossible without expert guidance:

Every spring, as hopeful climbers from around the world trek to Everest Base Camp (an elevation of about 17,500 feet in Nepal) to begin acclimating for a summit push in May, a team of local Sherpas is hired to create the season's route up the mountain. They establish the course up more than two vertical miles that hundreds will follow.

First, the "icefall doctors" set ropes, ladders and make-shift bridges through the notoriously dangerous, ever-shifting Khumbu Icefall immediately above Base Camp. Others keep moving upward, setting anchors and stringing ropes until they reach the summit. The process can take weeks, and is often delayed by bad weather.

Only when the ropes are fixed to the top does the Everest climbing season open.

—**John Branch,** *New York Times*[1]

The Sherpa are built for the climb—literally. They have a different type of physiology that allows them to still function at 100% while helping people summit. It is truly impressive to go up and down the mountain multiple times and stay alert in the midst of stress, weather and irrational people to help others climb.

"Sherpas are so adept at working hard at high altitudes because of a mysterious physiological trick their bodies pull off unseen anywhere else on Earth," according to Rasmus Nielsen, an expert on the biology of the Sherpa. "They seem to function well in high altitude without producing as many red blood cells and no one knows for sure why."[2]

Although climbing is hard enough for our own leader-ship journey, getting others to higher levels takes significant training and skill. What is true in climbing is true in leading. To get other people to the top, the following must be true:

- We actually want to help others be the best leaders they can be.
- We have gone to higher levels ourselves and have mastered the tools to help others climb.
- We have influence with others for them to want our help.
- They actually want to get to the next level and are prepared to put in the work to get there.
- We have the mentality to handle the stress and the difficulties along the way.

Taking Others to a Higher Place

Most of the leaders who help others don't get the credit they deserve, but that is not why they help others climb. "Some have climbed the world's tallest mountain a dozen times, risking their lives with every trek and getting little credit for it. All the people who are so famous for climbing Everest are white western climbers. Everybody forgets they didn't just go up by themselves . . . Sherpas are most critical to the success of a climb."[3]

As a Sherpa, you are the most critical factor in the success of others. Let's look at our next key tool, called Liberating Others (see Figure 6.1).

The goal of a 100X leader is to establish liberation, which is to fight for the highest possible good of those we lead—by using the intentional calibration of support and challenge. We must become adept at learning what specific support or challenge others need from us in the moment, whether they are our spouse or friends or team members. It is our job to calibrate that support and challenge so that they can move to the next level with the proper equipping and motivation.

> *The goal of a 100X leader is to liberate—to fight for the highest possible good of those they lead.*

Fight for the highest possible good in the lives of those they lead.

❶ What specific support and challenge do they need from me?

❷ What is the tendency or pattern most undermining their influence?

❸ How do I help them get to the next level?

GiANT WORLDWIDE   Source: Inspired by Kevin Weaver, REORIENT   © Pub House

Figure 6.1   Liberating Others
Source: © **Pub House/GiANT Worldwide**

Once this is established then your job is to look for what could take them out—the tendencies or patterns that undermine their influence. If you truly care for those you are leading then it is vital for you to bring honesty with respect, to speak the truth in love, in order for them to become the best they can be. Most people sadly never experience liberation and so your job as a 100X leader, or Sherpa, is to not shirk your responsibilities in order to liberate.

You are also responsible to help them see the future and the mountain ahead of them as you equip them to climb. This is the noble role of leadership—to be healthy, secure, and confident enough to help other people climb. We badly need these leaders, these true liberators, who choose to fight for the good of other people rather than simply themselves.

This story from one of our clients shows how to set up employees for success as they begin their journey of climbing inside the company.

My introduction to a new company involved a few video chats, a handful of text threads, and one memorable care package that had a couple of books inside; *5 Voices* and *5 Gears*. Our CEO described these resources as "the cornerstone of our culture and how we liberate and multiply." They set out a common language for liberation.

A few weeks and some late-night reading sessions later and I was sold. There was something different about this company and its values. When I joined the team, they were three years into their 100X journey. At first, it was a foreign and somewhat overwhelming world to enter into, but I quickly witnessed the fruit of adopting a common language and set of tools that proved to work for the betterment of the whole team.

The leaders weren't afraid to look at themselves and acknowledge their imperfections. And they were investing time and energy into discovering why they operated the way they did and how it impacted the people around them. As a person who enjoys self-exploration and the discovery of the "why" behind my thoughts and actions, I found this very refreshing.

I have watched people liberate others and have experienced others fighting for my highest possible good. I've learned that challenge from the mouth of someone who cares about you is not a personal attack, but a technique for sharpening and strengthening you. We need our friends, family, and teammates to help us see the things we cannot see or choose not to see for ourselves, the good and the bad.

That is what a Sherpa does. With balanced doses of support and challenge, my leaders instilled a new belief in myself.

To me, liberation means seeking ways to improve, grow, and positively impact those around you. Liberation is available for those willing to be in the arena, those striving for greatness, and those not afraid of failure as they relentlessly pursue being the best spouse, friend, family member, teammate, and leader they can be.

—**Paige Pulford, Executive Lead, TEAMTRI,**
Chattanooga, TN

Committing to Depth

The 100X leader commits to being with you for the long term, to lead in a way that shows they've truly taken the time to get to know you and understand the specific challenges you are dealing with in that moment. They look ahead and speak life into you while helping you deal with roadblocks or negative patterns.

To liberate others takes intentionality and a longer-term commitment than most leaders are prepared for, but this tenacity is the key to overcoming the impossible odds of climbing higher levels. There is no shortcut to the top of the mountain, whether you are climbing yourself or functioning as a Sherpa for others. That's why so few leaders function at the highest levels or help others do the same.

The 100X leader will climb with you and multiply their abilities by allowing you to imitate them. They say things like, "learn from me and as you mature you can innovate and go beyond my ability." That has to be the highest calling for any Sherpa—to give all they have so that others may eventually climb further and faster than they have done. That takes incredible security and humility!

Are you prepared to do the same for your people? Are you prepared to do everything you can to help them fulfill their potential and go even beyond you? Do you know their dreams and aspirations for the future? Are you prepared to help them climb to your level and then encourage them to go further?

These are the liberating leaders that will change the world. These are the leaders who will leave a legacy long after they have retired or passed on.

So, who are the three people you want or need to be a Sherpa for?

1. _____

2. _____

3. _____

Now ask the three questions from the Liberating Others tool:

1. What specific support and/or challenge do they need from me?
2. What is the tendency or pattern most undermining their influence?
3. How can I help them get to the next level?

How to Get People to Change

People change when they see what it is like to be on the other side of themselves. They begin to understand the damage they are causing and actually want to change themselves once they see there is a clear path to that change.

As Sherpas, our job is to help our people see the other side of themselves. It means having difficult conversations when necessary, while providing the right resources and support for your team, family, spouse, to become the best, healthiest, most productive version of themselves as they can.

Some of you might be doubting the capacity of adults to change at all, given their bad habits or set roles deeply ingrained over the course of a career. For those who lean toward that opinion, consider the following scenarios and think about the likelihood of change occurring in each situation:

Scenario 1:

John walks into his manager's office with a tinge of frustration. A co-worker has accused him of "poor use of words" to another colleague. The manager begins to berate John with yelling and threats. This was not the first episode with John and the manager has had enough. This is the final warning. The manager tells him that he will be watching him like a hawk, and if he does anything else to cause a disruption, there will be severe consequences.

What do you think the results will be? Do you think John is likely to change or begin getting along with his colleagues better? Do you think he'll change his perspective on his own behavior or his perception of his colleagues?

Scenario 2:

John walks into his manager's office with a tinge of frustration. A co-worker has accused him of "poor use of words" to another colleague. The manager begins to talk with John, "John, do you know that I am for you?" John looks wary.

The manager continues, "What is going on? What is causing you to hurt those around you, John?" As the conversation unfolds, the manager's questions and genuine concern form a figurative mirror in which John can see a reflection of himself and his actions. The mirror allows him to see—maybe for the first time—what it's actually like to be on the other side of him. It enables him to step into his colleagues' shoes and then begin to dig into the issues that are causing him to act and respond the way he does.

Now, what will the results be? Do you think John is more or less likely to change his perspective and behavior than in the first scenario? Do you think he might be more receptive to this approach from the manager?

Every person you take up the mountain must understand your intent and see it in your actions. They must understand that you are for them as you liberate and move yourself away from dominating, abdicating or protecting tendencies. They must value you and your influence in their life and you must stay with them long enough to see the chance for change and get to the next level.

One of our 100X tools is the Liberators Intent (see Figure 6.2). It is simple, but powerful with the axiom of "calling people up, not out," and we were inspired by the leader of Legacy School, Suzanne Phillips. She shared with a group of executives how kids change: "Children don't change by shaming them, they change through aspiration. You must call them up to who they are becoming instead of calling out their current behavior."

Her points hit home as all of us thought about our tendencies to call out our kids when they don't behave, as we would wish. She went on to share, "as parents our job is to show them who we see them to be and call them up to those standards by

Figure 6.2   The Liberator's Intent
Source: © Pub House/GiANT Worldwide

saying, 'Why are you acting like you are down here? We know who you are. You are a leader and have so much talent and skill. This is who you really are.'" Suzanne went on to teach the executives the positive psychological effects of using aspiration to help kids reach higher levels. We believe the same is true with the adults you lead. Call them higher and remind them who they are and watch them self-adjust. The other alternative is to call them out on what they are not becoming, which rarely produces what you hope. Positive change rarely comes from negative judgment.

> *Positive change rarely comes from negative judgment.*

The 100X leader wants those they lead to be empowered and to fulfill the potential they have as a human being and as a team member.

Why Being "For Others" Works

The truth is, we have seen the previous scenario 1 play out many times in real life during our work with clients. People like "John" have become used to causing pain and then suffering the berating that comes from those who lead them. It is a pattern that plays out everywhere, and in this scenario, nothing really changes. John just takes the heat, but then uses it to fuel the fire of anger inside him, resulting in resentment, continued poor conduct, and possibly even worse behavior as the me-versus-them mentality exacerbates the divide. When this happens, John feels orphaned by his team, believing no one is in his corner. Once he starts thinking, "no one is for me, I'll just do things my way," the pattern continues spiraling, and his victim mindset drives him to harm others in his path.

The alternate scenario, on the other hand, has more of a tendency to work for two reasons:

1. Showing You Are For Others

John's manager, in scenario 2, showed that they were *for* John. Being "*for*" someone means that you will work harder to try to help the other person, rather than simply yelling or disciplining them. It means that you care enough about their well-being that you'll set aside your own convenience and agenda to provide the support or challenge they need to grow. Sometimes there is simply nothing you can do and the person needs to be let go and move on to a better-fit elsewhere. Sometimes it means a lot of extra investment.

Regardless of the necessary action, when John knows that you are for him, you actually help break part of the ingrained pattern that has been holding him back and hurting his influence. He doesn't know the "I'm-for-you" script because he has never seen this approach before. He's never had to respond to an attitude that doesn't make it him vs. you, but instead recasts the two of you as partners in figuring things out for his highest possible good and benefit. That in itself has the chance to truly impact him for the better.

2. Holding Up the Mirror

The biggest opportunity for change comes from actually holding up the metaphorical mirror and seeking to draw out their perspective and understanding. When a person sees himself or herself in a mirror, they have the choice to change. In general, most people don't want to be known as jerks or lazy or whatever issues others seem to have with them.

If someone is told their faults bluntly, they can become defensive and reject it. But when someone who is fighting for their highest possible good reflects back to them, they are more apt to recognize the problem and take the initiative to change. It's the difference between telling someone a truth, versus guiding them in their own journey to find it.

That's why deep, lasting change in a person happens from the inside. Sherpas need a great deal of patience, a "for-others" attitude, and a commitment to learning how to bring both high support and high challenge with precision.

If you keep these two scenarios in mind and work to apply the mirror and "for-others" mindset, you'll be surprised at how quickly your capacity expands in order to cultivate change in those you lead.

The Secret to Transformation

Do you really want to help others climb beyond what they ever believed was possible, to the higher levels? This only happens through transformation and, like metamorphosis, transformation is a process requiring your guidance if people are going to experience a dramatic change in their life.

We created GiANT Worldwide to give people the platform of leadership to raise up liberating leaders in every city and sector to change their own leadership culture, with the hope that it will spread throughout the world. Our senior consultants and partners work tirelessly around the globe as Sherpas for others on the 100X journey toward liberation.

As Steve and I (Jeremie) were building our company's framework we found that the secret to significant transformation happened through three primary elements:

1. **Restoration:** Restoration of people to who they truly are by helping them understand their very nature—their personality and wiring. We found that for leaders to be 100% healthy, they needed to experience a kind of healing. Healing can come from the act of forgiveness of a parent or coach or friend. At other times healing can look like the overcoming of your own harsh tendency to dominate yourself. Healing restores people to the good health they need to climb at higher levels. It is what is needed to become secure and confident on the journey.

2. **Taking Out:** Every leader must stop doing certain things in order to become their best selves. This is often the hardest element of climbing. It is the stripping off of bad habits, the ceasing of negative mindsets and the change in language or treatment of another. We use the Know Yourself to Lead Yourself tool to help leaders see it themselves, and then we help them get rid of the patterns that are keeping them from having significant influence like a plant that needs to be pruned to grow.

3. **Raising Up:** As mentioned earlier, we remind people who they are and can be, and then we fight for their highest

good to get to that level. Every one of us has so much more potential than we know, but most have settled into the rut of everyday living while our view of ourselves has dissipated in the tasks of daily work. As Sherpas it is crucial to reconnect our people with their dreams of what they could be—to expand their horizons and look upward.

This is the framework we have built our business upon and we want to help you do the same as a Sherpa:

- To calibrate high support and high challenge as you lead others.
- To fight for the highest possible good of those you lead.
- To help people get rid of the things that are limiting them.
- To help them understand their passions/dreams.
- To call people up, not out.
- To acclimate people and teach them to multiply what they know to those they serve.

When It's Time to Fight

Some of you are deathly afraid of fighting—of challenging people to get to the next level. It may feel like conflict to some of you, when in reality it is a catalyst to breakthrough, which every leader needs. Fighting in this context means fighting for the highest possible good in others—the definition of love. It aims to call people up, not tear people down.

So, what about you? Are you willing to make the hard calls when you know it is right? Or, are you putting it off for another week, month, quarter, or year because you are afraid of the people you are trying to help?

- Are you ready to help someone who is afraid of the future find a more fitting role, even if it's outside your organization?
- Are you willing to help someone through the self-awareness process of seeing the broccoli in their teeth and helping them get it out?
- Can you muster the strength to share with someone the thing that everyone else but them knows they need to change?
- Is it time to fight for a relationship to make it what it really should be?
- Are you willing to push people to think bigger and act better when they undermine themselves?

We love the word *fight* because it normally has a negative connotation. However, when you truly fight for a person's highest possible good, then fighting becomes a positive. What might this look like specifically?

- Bringing strong direct challenge to a leader who is having paranoid thoughts and explaining that they are actually insecure.
- You may have a family member whose moods affect the entire family. To break the pattern, it must be addressed in love, by fighting for them to get the help they need instead of continuing to sweep issues under the rug.
- A co-worker may have a habit that is really affecting his or her future. To fight for his or her highest possible good would be to help them confront it, deal with it, and overcome it. He or she might choose to resent you for a while, but if you allow them to stay with that habit, you choose to limit his or her future.
- Fighting may look like rolling up your sleeves to help someone on a project that they messed up on and training them to improve as you fix their mistake.

Here is what fighting can look like from the employee's perspective:

I have noticed a shift in how our leader operates because of the Support-Challenge Matrix. Rather than over-supporting, now he brings challenge to our team consistently. The challenge comes in different ways ranging from him asking thoughtful questions that lead our team to pause, think, and go back and try again, to a more direct approach, where he is getting specific about expectations and opportunities for growth.

At one time, I was struggling in finding my place on our team. I was challenged by our leader to pause, think, and process. He also encouraged (supported) me to look at the Matrix to see how I could liberate myself. He asked me to think about how I could support myself by not being so self-critical and challenge myself by making more of a commitment to working out my own preferred future plan. This was something that I was not doing, and I needed someone to call me up, not out. He did.

Seeing how liberation can be applied to all Circles of Influence, including self, was liberating and led me to a transformational moment in my own life. I don't think I would be a part of this team here today if it weren't for that key moment in my leadership journey.

—Danielle Tolentino Tuason, VP of Leadership Innovation, Orange County, California

Most people want others to change, but rarely are willing to help them because they are simply more focused on themselves. If you want to be a Sherpa for someone, then that means that you are willing to fight for the highest possible good in that person—for the greater good!

Learning to Fight When You Are Used to Serving

This leader works for one of our clients in Romania. She is so talented and has been on the 100X leader journey for a number of years. Hear how she describes her journey to "fighting for another's good" when she had only been used to serving:

> I just love people. I now know my mission in life—it's to genuinely help people grow themselves. At work especially, I used to frequently be told that I was protecting my team. That pissed me off, as in my mind I didn't do that; instead, I was always just encouraging my team for how hard they were working to deliver results. What I didn't know was that I was afraid to bring challenge because I didn't know how to do that effectively without being perceived as a dominator and losing people's trust.
>
> I'm learning how to really lead others now by liberating them and I can celebrate these tangible breakthroughs:
>
> - Bringing a challenge is actually beneficial and empowering to the team. Sometimes we don't even realize we need a challenge instead of support.
> - Bringing a challenge doesn't mean you don't love those people, it means we actually care enough that we want them to genuinely succeed as leaders.
> - Investing time and discipline in calibrating support and challenge in the way we behave as leaders is the biggest gift we can offer to ourselves.
>
> **—Adriana Turcanu, HR Business Partner,**
> **Endava Central Europe**

This might be you—the person who needs to learn to fight in order to become someone people want to follow.

Maybe that is you, the one who needs to learn how to take others up the mountain. You just needed a nudge and a reminder of a higher way to lead. We need more fighters who are servants. That sounds weird, we know! Servant fighters. That is what a 100X leader is—a Sherpa who liberates as a lifestyle.

Taking others up the mountain is possible even when the landscape looks impossible. Even if you are leading dysfunctional kids, know it is possible.

Even when a team looks distracted and doesn't want to climb, know there is a way.

When an organization is upside down, know there is a way to turn it around. It takes time and intentionality and consistency to develop them to their potential. You must then set the right expectations while you fight for the highest possible good for them.

Notes

1. John Branch, "Deliverance From 27,000 Feet," *New York Times*, December 19, 2017.
2. Rasmus Nielsen, biology professor (Sherpas' genealogical makeup), University of California, Berkeley, quoted in Rick Jervis, "Sherpas Are Way of Life for Treacherous Climbs," *USA Today*, April 21, 2014.
3. Laura Mallonee, "The Overlooked Heroes Who Lead Climbers Up Everest," *Wired*, August 2017.

7 | Developing Others and Managing Expectations

You cannot be a good mountaineer, however great your ability, unless you are cheerful and have the spirit of comradeship. Friends are as important as achievement. Teamwork is the one key to success and selfishness only makes a man small. No man, on a mountain or elsewhere, gets more out of anything than he puts into it.
— Tenzing Norgay (who along with Edmund Hillary was one of the first two individuals to successfully summit Mount Everest on May 29, 1953)

These words of wisdom describe the life of the 100X leader—a healthy spirit with a desire to help others and put the work into becoming this type of leader.

We have found that when you give yourself to help the right people you will experience a rich and rewarding life. To liberate is to free others and with that freedom usually comes the recognition and honor that fuels the 100X leader to do it again and again.

The Legacy of a 100X Life

The intentional life creates a legacy that is significant and memorable. Here is Steve's vision for his life and his legacy:

I imagine I'm at the end of my life with only a few weeks left and it's time to say my goodbyes. The question I often ask myself is how many people would take the time to travel in order to say goodbye in person. How many lives have I been able to influence to such a degree that they would do more than send an email or social media message? This to me is the true 100X leader test. When you multiply knowledge, skills, and expertise into the life of another it's an investment that only grows over time. We always remember the leaders who helped us climb to levels we never believed possible ourselves. That will be for me the true measure of the life I've lived, it's what gets me out of bed in the morning and why I'm committed to liberate all I can.

What is your dream? What do you want your legacy to be?

Developing Others

In this chapter we want to show you how to develop your people. We truly believe that people are assets, not liabilities, if given the time, energy, and support to help them grow.

When developing others, it is important to have a framework to understand where you are in the process with the person you are developing. We have modified the Hierarchy of Competence as our framework for describing the process of development. An employee, Noel Burch, developed this theory—frequently attributed to Abraham Maslow—at Gordon International Training in the 1970s.[1]

First let's remind ourselves of the Hierarchy of Competence.

Stage One: **Unconscious Incompetence**—This is when a person is clueless and they don't realize it. They may not believe the skill that they are doing is important and thus they can discount any counsel or training. In order to get to the next level, a person must own the reality that they don't understand what they are being asked to learn.

Stage Two: **Conscious Incompetence**—This painful stage occurs when a person realizes their deficiency and has a choice to learn through their mistakes on the quest to becoming competent or "faking it until they make it," in order to not be viewed as incompetent.

Stage Three: **Conscious Competence**—This is the stage of breakthrough when a person becomes good at a task and can consistently do it, though it does require concentration.

Stage Four: **Unconscious Competence**—This is the stage when a person masters a craft or task in such a skilled way that it becomes second nature and they are so familiar with it that they do it without thinking, even multitasking at the same time.

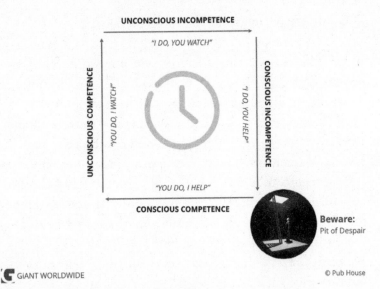

Figure 7.1 Developing Others
Source: A. Maslow, Gordon Training International. © Pub House/GiANT Worldwide.

We have innovated this model (see Figure 7.1), having highlighted a potential pitfall (the pit of despair, which we'll go into later), which could happen between the conscious incompetence and conscious competence stages.

Now that you have the general framework, let's move on to the practicalities of developing others by liberating them and fighting for their highest possible good. If you want to be a 100X leader, then you need to understand the different stages and adapt them based on where the person is at that moment. This will take time and you will need patience and commitment through the process of helping them to conscious competence. Depending on the complexity of the role you are trying to multiply, it will take a long time to properly reach unconscious competence.

So, as a working example, choose a person in your mind who you want to get to the next level and plan how you could walk them through the Developing Others tool discussed earlier.

As soon as they have realized they are unconsciously incompetent, you want to move them onto the next stage quickly. Agree on your plan of action, and start to intentionally show them how to accomplish a project you desire to complete, encouraging them to help you. This feels like a lot of challenge, but you will be functioning as a 100X leader. Anything looks really easy when done by someone who is unconsciously competent in it!

There are a number of variables that will help you develop them to this stage. Normally, higher levels of jobs bring with them the expectation of higher levels of competency and a lack of hands on training process. The real issue then is the tendency of all directors and/or executives to start to question whether they've made the right hire when something goes wrong. Sherpas who understand the process know that when the person they are investing in is in conscious incompetence, that's when they most need to know their Sherpa is 100% committed to getting them up the mountain. Being able to describe their reality using a visual tool helps them understand that any frustration or feelings of inadequacy are a natural part of the process (see Figure 7.2). Unlike the average leader, unaware of this stage or its dangers, the Sherpa has made this journey before and can be trusted with the climb before them.

Every employee needs a breakthrough, and 100X leaders look for the breakthrough moments and celebrate them as they help people on this journey of growth. Celebrate the small wins particularly when the person experiences even a glimpse of conscious competence!

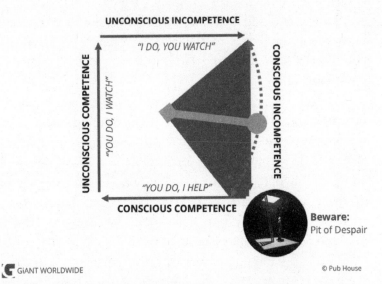

UNCONSCIOUS INCOMPETENCE

"I DO, YOU WATCH"

CONSCIOUS INCOMPETENCE

"YOU DO, I WATCH"

UNCONSCIOUS COMPETENCE

"YOU DO, I HELP"

CONSCIOUS COMPETENCE

Beware:
Pit of Despair

GiANT WORLDWIDE   © Pub House

**Figure 7.2   The Breakthrough Moment from
Unconsciously Incompetent to Consciously Incompetent**
Source: A. Maslow, Gordon Training International. © Pub
House/GiANT Worldwide.

Who was the leader who helped you climb to the next level? How did they help you along the way? How patient were they with you?

What would our world look like if we had millions of liberators who were developing others intentionally? What if we had leaders who were allowing others to learn from their unconscious competence, sharing their magic? We believe this process could radically improve working life for teams and individuals everywhere.

The problem is that there are days when these employees will drive you crazy as they pendulum back from conscious competence to conscious incompetence (see Figure 7.3). It might feel like two steps forward, one step back, but you know that as a liberating leader your job is to calibrate high support and high

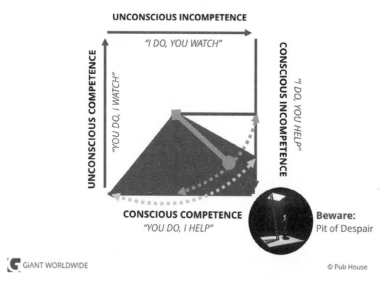

Figure 7.3   Increasing Conscious Competence
Source: **A. Maslow, Gordon Training International. ©
Pub House/GiANT Worldwide.**

challenge to show them where they need to grow and to fight
for them to get to the next level. As they reach the bottom of
the right corner they need very little challenge, they are doing
enough of that themselves. That is often where they need maximum support to keep going. At the turn, they will have lost
much of their self-confidence, they are only sticking at it because
you believe in them and despite their protestations, you continue
to invest in them and tell them they will make it.

The pit of despair is full of people whose leader gave up on
them somewhere along the leadership journey in the conscious
incompetence stage and have moved on without them. In truth,
there is no way around the corner without a dedicated Sherpa.

If a person does fall into the pit of despair they usually land,
then look around and nod at the others who have already made
the pit their home. As they drink their coffee they say things like,

"Hey Bob, how long have you been down here?" Bob then goes on to tell his story of neglect, while sharing some gossip and cynicism about a certain leader and the company as a whole. The new inhabitant of the pit of despair begins to make it his or her home too and a new depressing and negative norm is established.

There are millions of employees in companies around the world who go to work every day in the pit of despair! The art of being a 100X leader is the ability to lead people consistently around the bottom right corner of the square (see Figure 7.4). People only fall into the pit when their Sherpa has given up on them. And when that happens they give up on themselves, creating a cycle of failure.

Most leaders don't like being around conscious incompetence. They start to believe they made the wrong hire, or think they've invested in the wrong person and they withdraw their support just at the time the person most needs their Sherpa.

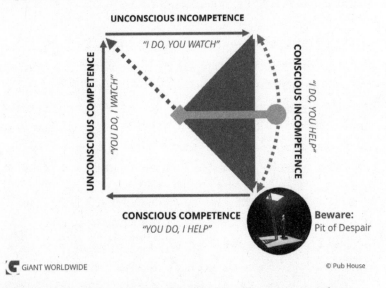

Figure 7.4 The pit of despair is a dangerous place.
Source: **A. Maslow, Gordon Training International. ©
Pub House/GiANT Worldwide.**

Here are three things the 100X leader must provide to keep people out of the pit of despair:

1. **Time**—Your people need both informal and formal time to help them out of this pit. Informal time, in that they need the casual connection with you that builds trust and helps them acclimate to you and your leadership style. And formal time, in that they need clear direction and expectations about how they succeed in their jobs. Right now, they feel they are inadequate to the task and are teetering on the brink of the pit—you will need to patiently talk them up and out of it.

2. **Vision**—Your people need to know that their personal vision matches the company's long-term vision. Do they really belong? If so, you must help them reach that conclusion and begin the climb back up to productivity. Keep reminding them of the long-term goal—to become fully competent.

3. **Encouragement**—Your people need your specific encouragement, not just generic encouragement. Find ways to encourage them to conscious competence.

Paul Drange, Director at Sourcewell, describes the ways he has changed his development of others:

Before encountering the 100X Leader framework, I was simply managing my department and people by feel and past experience. Then the Support-Challenge Matrix really changed the way I develop people. I tended to protect my team and was really good at giving support—almost to a fault. What I wasn't effective at was bringing the correct amount of challenge so that they realized what it was like to be their true best self. Thus, I didn't help them to develop as fully as they could have been. This change helped me do two key things—build deeper and longer lasting trust with my staff and organization, and realize the highest, most true potential for my staff and for myself.

To become consistent in your liberation as a 100X leader you must be consistent in your calibration of high support and high challenge to enable people to make the transition from conscious incompetence to conscious competence. Once this is taking place consistently, the individual will become unconsciously competent through time and repetition as they master their role or task.

It is possible to get your team members around the square. The secret to developing others is your willingness to actually do the development work.

> *The secret to developing others is your willingness to actually do the development work.*

Of course, you must have made your own journey from unconscious incompetence to unconscious competence. As a Sherpa, you will already be acclimated so that people see you leading yourself well first and only then will they allow you to influence them. That journey has no shortcuts but instead requires much effort on your own journey to gain the respect needed to help others climb.

If you want more details on how to develop others, we have created a thorough digital process for you, and details on how to access this are found at the back of this book.

A key to developing others is learning to master expectations, both your own and those you are leading. Success has everything to do with clarifying what you expect from others and what they expect of you. The Sherpa and the climber both know exactly where they are headed, and what they expect from each other.

Managing Expectations

When expectations are unmet, this eventually leads to resentment, bitterness, and settling for a new, lower norm in a relationship. For instance, if someone in your life has expectations of you that are not reasonable, but never shares them with you, both you and the other party are going to be frustrated.

In our work with leaders, teams, and people in general we continue to see that much of the drama that people experience comes from the mismanagement of expectations and this mismanagement affects relationships and communication in ways that could have been entirely avoided.

Expectations are strong beliefs concerning what people ought or should be doing. All of us have expectations (see Figure 7.5). It is impossible not to have them. However, it is the way we manage and communicate them that make us more effective in leading people up the mountain.

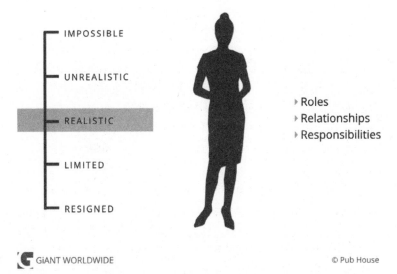

Figure 7.5   Expectations Scale
Source: © **Pub House/GiANT Worldwide.**

There are some personality types that yield impossible expectations. These people, who normally tend to dominate others, are constantly pushing others to the brink with their high expectations. We have found that many venture capital firms and hired gun CEOs will create impossible expectations as a strategy, knowing that their people won't hit these goals, but that they will be higher than they would have set for themselves. This type of strategy is brutal as it burns people out and then replaces them when they can no longer cope with the stress.

The next level is unrealistic expectations and again, most of us will have these in relation to something in our lives, whether it is new employees, our next vacation, or the latest gadget. Protecting leaders (low challenge, high support) tend to have unrealistic expectations but rarely share them, which create cultures of entitlement or mistrust because of their lack of communication.

Obviously, the ideal is to have and communicate realistic expectations, but to achieve this is rare. If we could all learn how to have truly realistic expectations within our relationships, roles, and responsibilities, then we would increase our influence and effectiveness, not to mention sleep better at night. It is important to truly analyze our expectations in relation to others. Are they limited? Resigned? Most people simply haven't understood their expectations or haven't shared them appropriately. If we have not actually communicated our expectations, and people respond to us in a different way than we had hoped, then we become resigned or apathetic in our expectations. Assuming people understand what is expected usually ends in disappointment.

Take some time to reflect on the Expectations Scale for your various relationships, roles, and responsibilities.

Expectations Exercise

If you want to get to the next level as a 100X leader, then here is an exercise you can do to better manage your expectations.

1. List three people in your life for whom you have expectations. This could be your work colleagues, friend, partner, or child.
2. What are the expectations that you have for each of these people? Be as specific as you can.
3. Do they know what your expectations are? How would they know? Have you made any unfair assumptions?
4. Are your expectations for them impossible, unrealistic, realistic, limited, or resigned? Are they meeting your expectations? If not, why do you think that is?

Reflect on how you could start to be clearer in sharing your expectations and the liberation, which could happen if you intentionally did this with the people in your life. Do the hard work and you will be glad you did.

Have You Actually Told Them?

Years ago I (Jeremie) had a conversation with an executive who described in detail his frustration about one of his leaders, a vice president who wasn't getting it. The CEO was upset as he described in detail what his vice president was or wasn't doing with the people he was leading.

As I listened to him, a couple of questions bubbled to the top of my mind.

First, I asked him, "So, why is he still on your team?" He shared with exasperation that the guy held a certain competency that was hard to find. This VP couldn't connect with others, was a horrible communicator, and was always defensive according to the CEO. However, he was the best in the industry in his field and they needed his competency and reputation. [Side note—we hear this almost every time we talk with a CEO about a specific person on their team. Someone is toxic to the team culture but is too valuable to let go because of certain competency or industry knowledge. It is a catch-22 most of the time]. The next question threw him for a curve. "Have you told him?" I was simply asking, "Have you explained your frustrations, discussed what it is like to be on the other side of him, and worked with him to challenge him to be the leader you want him to be?"

The CEO looked at me, stunned as his mind was processing the question. It had never occurred to him to share his expectations with the vice president. His response was, "Well I need him to be on the team and so we just put up with him, but we don't know how much longer we can do that. If I told him what I think he would get so defensive. So, I just work around him."

The CEO was allowing this vice president to lead the whole culture of his division. The executive wasn't challenging, but rather hinting. He wasn't confronting because he was afraid of losing his technical skillset and so he just put up with the drama and worked around it with the other executives who felt the same way. This vice president was a drain on everyone around him but held a power card of experience and industry knowledge like blackmail over the company. The CEO chose not to share his reasonable expectations and never found out how the VP would have responded. Years later the VP jumped to a bigger opportunity, trading on his skillset, but never understood what it was truly like to work on the other side of himself.

If you are having issues with someone on your team but haven't provided the appropriate challenge with support, then you are abdicating your role for that person and your responsibility to the team. If you really want the best for the other person and the team, then fight for the highest possible good of the difficult person and clarify your reasonable expectations with him or her, face to face.

Remember, if you are the leader of a team with responsibility then you are the culture keeper. A Sherpa would not allow one climber to steer the direction of the entire team just because of that person's ego. If you abdicate it to the person you are afraid of confronting, then you have created the culture that you are trapped in today. We're going to talk more about the vital area of setting culture in Chapter 9.

Do the right thing—share your expectations. Tell them where they really stand. It isn't fair for that person to continue to do what they are doing simply because they are unaware of the drama they are spreading. Tell them and liberate those you lead. Write your expectations down and share them with your team so there is total clarity. Give them the opportunity to grow—that's what a Sherpa does.

How to Properly Manage Expectations and Save Yourself from Grief

Now let's get even more practical. Whenever you find conflict you will find unmet expectations and poor communication. A promise was broken or unmet.

So, here is a possible resolution worth considering. Whenever you establish anything new, immediately draft your expectations and then share them with the parties you are partnering with or with coworkers, and so forth.

It might possibly look like this from a team leader:

Managing Expectations: The XYZ Project

We expect Gemini Company to help us modify our software solutions so that we can do X, Y, and Z within 90 days as promised. I expect them to be considerate and easy to work with because that is what they promised. If we can get this accomplished I will be more than happy with the project.

Signed, Susan Smith

We know that is normally what contracts are for, but quite frankly, contracts look more like congressional bills than a statement of expectation. If you were to state your expectations clearly, print it and give both parties a copy then we would probably have fewer issues in our lives and fewer legal bills to pay.

Here is what it might look like *within* a company:

Managing Expectations: Internal Growth Initiative for the R&D Study

We expect to get a suitable answer to our problem around X by working with three internal groups with a deadline of two weeks. To do that we need to meet at least three times. We expect to hit this deadline because by doing this we believe it will help the company do . . .

Signed, Bill Smith

You may find that this works so well that you simply begin to write down all your expectations so that you learn to externalize them more effectively.

Managing Expectations in All Our Circles of Influence

We all have expectations of those in our circles—ourselves, our family, team, community, and organization. The problem with most of us is that we rarely share anything externally (whether verbally or written) to others and thus, they tend to have no idea that they didn't meet our expectations. They are perplexed at our passive-aggressive nature and don't realize that they are being set to a standard that they know nothing about!

One couple, Greg and Tracy Rader, have worked diligently on resetting expectations in their marriage after they first saw the Expectations Scale tool at one of our GiANT Liberator Network retreats. This is their "aha":

> We realized that because of our personality wiring we were missing each other and that our expectations were unmet in a few areas of our life. We had become accidental in our marriage and so our communication became a bit static. As a couple we decided to become more intentional and begin to fight for each other's highest possible good. A key to this was committing to practice communicating our expectations as we found that any disappointment came because we weren't sharing those properly, which had resulted in resentment or resignation. It's made a huge difference.

Eliminate drama by sharing expectations. Place them on the Expectations Scale and if they are not reasonable, change them!

Eliminate drama by sharing expectations.

Holding People Accountable while You Develop Them

As Sherpas, your job is to help people become consciously competent to keep them from falling into the pit of despair. We've just discussed the importance of communicating reasonable expectations. But what happens if the people you lead still don't perform to the higher standard you need them to? How do you keep people accountable?

> I believe that the traditional performance review process of reviewing performance once per year around salary discussions is the least effective model for raising individual performance. Instead, I believe the most effective method to hold employees accountable and to drive performance is to create an ongoing conversation around continuous improvement. If an employee knows where they are at any given time, and they have someone walking with them in the process then their success will go up tenfold. By using the GiANT tools, we have given our leaders the language and the visuals to help coach those they lead to become leaders worth following. That is how it works—consistent leadership on a regular basis, not just an annual "hit and run."
>
> **—Deanna Farmer, CAO, Enable Midstream**

We have certainly found that making continuous performance review into an ongoing conversation is the best way to hold people accountable while developing them. Figure 7.6 shows a tool to help understand what the real issues might be if you do find people who are continually underperforming.

Work through the performance diagnostic by asking yourself these questions from the top down in relation to

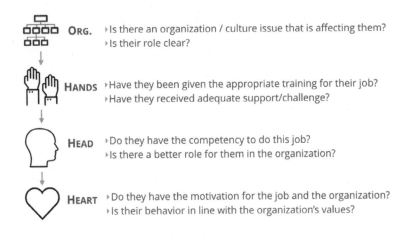

ORG.
▸ Is there an organization / culture issue that is affecting them?
▸ Is their role clear?

HANDS
▸ Have they been given the appropriate training for their job?
▸ Have they received adequate support/challenge?

HEAD
▸ Do they have the competency to do this job?
▸ Is there a better role for them in the organization?

HEART
▸ Do they have the motivation for the job and the organization?
▸ Is their behavior in line with the organization's values?

GiANT WORLDWIDE   Source: Influenced by Mark Herringshaw   © Pub House

Figure 7.6   Performance Diagnostic Tool
Source: © **Pub House/GiANT Worldwide.**

an employee who is not performing at the required level of expectation.

First, is there an organizational or cultural issue that is affecting that person? If not, move on to the next question. Is his or her role clear? If it is, move to the next questions until you conclude what you think the issue is. You are simply moving down from top to bottom starting with the organization first before analyzing the individual.

The hands section details your responsibility. Has the individual been given the appropriate training for the job? Have you properly shared your expectations? Has he or she heard and understood them? And has he or she received adequate support/challenge? Again, if the answer is yes to all these, keep moving on through the questions until you find the issue. Remember, your job as a Sherpa is to help the individual get to the next level.

Does the person have the competency to do this job? Is there a better role for him or her inside the organization? If the answer is no to both, then the individual may not be a part of the future team and your game plan must be developed to address this. This may seem like strong language, but the reality is that leaders must calibrate support and challenge and there are times when the challenge may be more pronounced if the performance is not meeting expectations.

Does he or she have the motivation for the job and belief in the organization? Is the person's behavior in line with the company's values? If there's finally a no here, the lack of passion affecting the individual's performance could be a personal issue that is bleeding over to work or maybe a character issue that needs to be addressed. Sometimes there are issues going on in the home that can affect a person's performance. Just remember the combination of grace and truth, of support and challenge. Be careful not to judge the person, but instead use this tool to help solve what is really going on with the person who is underperforming.

Here is how Tom Bell, CEO of Bell Lumber & Pole, does performance reviews on a regular basis:

We frame our performance reviews as coaching conversations. Specifically, we train supervisors to open their discussion of employee performance with the concept of Liberation—that the supervisor is "for" the supervisee, wanting to provide their direct reports with the right balance of challenge and support, to call up the employee's best work. Supervisors end the coaching conversation with an agreed written plan that specifies exactly what challenge and support will look like moving forward into the next review period.

It takes commitment to a system and to ongoing, consistent conversations that will take people to the next level. This diagnostic, together with all the other 100X tools we've looked at, can be used to work their way into the company culture. It is much easier for people to handle accountability and performance issues when they have consistent language and tools to help train supervisors and leaders throughout the organization.

To develop people is the beginning of the X, multiplication. It begins by being intentional and learning to share your expectations clearly while holding people accountable to the goal. In the next chapter, we want to share with you how to do what very few do—become a multiplication master.

Once you believe this then you can begin to take people to the higher levels and begin to learn how to master multiplication. And multiplying leaders are the top 1% on the planet.

Note

1. Hierarchy of Competence Theory, "Learning a New Skill Is Easier Said Than Done," Gordon Training International.

8 | Becoming a Multiplication Master

Some leaders divide, while others subtract.
Some will add, but the best leaders multiply.
—A GiANT axiom

What is specifically noble about the Sherpa is that most of them are not concerned about how many times they have summited Mount Everest. John Beede, our mountain climber from Chapter 1, explains it like this, "if you ask them, the Sherpa might be able to tell you how many times they have climbed to the top. However, what they are most proud of is how many clients they have helped summit. They know the exact number, whether it's '8 or 10 or 16' when referring to the success they have helped others achieve."

The Sherpa trust each other and believe the best in those they are serving. They can, however, burn out if the vision that they have for their clients is larger than the clients' own. Although the Sherpa can guide, carry, encourage, and climb up and down to help, they simply cannot carry or drag an unwilling or unmotivated climber to the top. The climber needs to have the same motivation as the Sherpa in order to succeed, and the 100X leader works on motivation as well as acclimation.

Therefore, it is the job of the 100X leader to observe when negative voices take over or when someone on their team lacks focus or even when there is pride or arrogance that could affect the group. And they multiply what they know to help those they are leading, but what is multiplication?

Intentional Multiplication

Multiplication is the intentional transfer of knowledge, skills, and expertise into the lives of the people you lead.

Multiplication is the intentional transfer of knowledge, skills, and expertise into the lives of the people you lead. If you become an expert in the art of multiplication, the capacity of the individual, team, and organization increases dramatically. The key is being intentional.

If leaders are accidental and abdicate their leadership, they may subtract, or worse, divide those they lead. Most of us have experienced this in certain leaders we have worked with, whether it be in the constant feeling of disappointment amid no expectations being shared or the dysfunctional leader who pits people against others as a sick game to try to produce competition that might increase performance. The 100X leader only multiplies the positive and does not subtract from people or divide teams.

The Sherpa are always training their clients as they climb, because they want the climber to be successful and not cause any issues for the team. Thus, they are constantly teaching rope mastery, climbing technique, coaching on the terrain, or whatever is helpful for the next challenge. In the same spirit, the 100X leader is looking to intentionally multiply what they know to those they are leading to get to higher levels.

Multiplying Magic

According to the Ecology Global Network, 151,600 people die every day in the world. How many of them transferred their collective knowledge, wisdom, or skills to others?

That is the problem. Each of us has certain magic inside of us that usually dies with us. There are two issues with this reality. One, most people have lived accidentally and didn't think about how or to whom to transfer their magic. Two, there are very few people asking to receive the magic that someone else has or had. Why is this? So much could be transferred but isn't.

Could it be that Siri and Alexa have become our source for knowledge, while we allow the skills of many to leave us forever? We all have so much to offer, so much to give, and yet the magic tends to stay locked inside.

There is an entire industry of wealth professionals that help people learn how to transfer their gold, but only a few of us that are

> *Wealth professionals help people learn how to transfer their gold, but only a few of us are trained to help people transfer their magic.*

trained to help people transfer their magic. Gold is much easier to transfer, because it is the tangible wealth from one person to another. There are dozens of ways to transfer money to others in the form of inheritance or gifts or donor advised funds, and so on. What if there were equal intentionality to learn all we can from those that are going before us? There is magic there, but most just choose to focus on the gold.

Not Renzi Stone. Renzi is an intentional leader. He runs a regional communications firm called Saxum and is one of the global board members of YPO (Young Professional Organization). He became so inspired by the concept of multiplying magic that he decided to implement a process with us that would radically affect his business and the way he leads. He also had a crazy idea that would become a deadline to truly multiply his knowledge, wisdom, skills, and expertise into his management team.

Renzi decided that he wanted to take his family on a global trip—for nine months. After leading his company for 15 years, he wanted to use the trip to raise the level of his leaders. If he couldn't leave, then he hadn't created the culture without himself. Thus, he had a few phases to ensure that the process worked:

Phase One—Prepare the team for the reality of the change and for the leadership changes.

Phase Two—Commence an intentional transfer of magic to multiple people around sales, operations, and customer service.

Phase Three—Lead from a distance and hope the plan works!

During phase one, we interviewed Renzi, his assistant, and other key leaders along with his wife, Lee Anne, to find out what Renzi did that no one else could do in the organization. We chose one of our GiANTs, Mickie Lara, to be the Sherpa to help this organization multiply their skills and expand their capacity.

Through phase two the team held core groups where leaders learned how to add these skill sets and practical applied learning sessions. Listen to how Renzi explains the process here:

> There is joy to be discovered when you invest in the success of others. Early in my career, I worried about the risk of passing along knowledge to others that would create a future competitor or worse, someone who would end up better at what I do than me. Age has a way of giving us perspective, which we hopefully turn into wisdom. I realized that training someone to be better than me was actually the highest, best use of my time to the company.
>
> As I prepared to leave the day-to-day physical presence in my company I had to be honest about what skills—magic— I had not fully transferred to others. I wanted them to know how I have grown the business. It was very difficult. Over the course of many weeks, I was able to share the tips and tricks I have used over the course of my 20-year career. Most of this was done in groups.
>
> Multiplying magic is not easy. The ancient Egyptians were the first to practice magic. The ancient practice is mainly tricks and tips passed down through the years to a select few. The beauty of the time we live in today is that information is accessible. Don't be the guy or girl who keeps it all for yourself.

What if every leader intentionally transferred their magic? What if every team learned to transfer their magic down

What if people paid as much attention to multiplying magic as they do in transferring gold?

throughout the organization, allowing skills and expertise to trickle down throughout the people?

What if people paid as much attention to multiplying magic as they do in transferring gold?

Four Ways to Multiply

Intentionally transferring knowledge, wisdom, or skills can look different in every organization to every leader. Communication is the key. Although some leaders love the newsletter or an e-mail, others value the in-depth one-to-one nature of coaching or apprenticeship. The truth is, there are many ways to multiply what you know to those you lead, and if you want to become a multiplication master you must understand the differences of each approach and become competent at each of them. Here are the four main methods of multiplying yourself into others.

Informing

Communication is critical for any leader and informing is the most traditional style of intentionally transferring knowledge, wisdom, or skills. This comes when a leader shares information in a one-way manner. For the Sherpa this occurs when they share rules or objectives or plans. For some leaders this occurs through a written newsletter or e-mail where they control what is communicated to others. For others, informing looks like the company speech or keynote where the leader is engaging through multiple channels with little or no interactive process.

Informing is important and valuable for multiplication, but most leaders think they are far more accomplished at informing than they actually are. It is genuinely hard to speak well in public and hold an audience, it's hard to craft e-mails or articles that capture precisely what you are trying to say succinctly and clearly and in the right tone.

The return on investment for this style of communication includes:

- Consistency, where everyone (hopefully) hears the same carefully crafted message.
- Efficiency, where repeatable mass communication can maximize a leader's time.
- Inspiration, where a good communicator can create employee engagement and buy in to the future vision.

It is important for leaders to understand the incredible power of informing if done well. The ROI is worth the effort but it is important to get real feedback on your current level of performance. This is where a Sherpa comes in handy, they will speak the truth in love, often in a way that your PA or team won't.

Training

Multiplying via training occurs by creating facilitated learning events with clearly defined objectives using a controlled interactive process. The most effective training occurs in groups of 15–25, but can stretch as high as 50 people, although the long-term ROI diminishes as the level of genuine interaction declines.

Training requires a different skillset in the interactive process. It is one thing to inform people and another to train.

The skillset is real and can be very effective to obtain buy-in inside the organization. Some leaders are natural at this and many are not at all. Designing a training experience is a skill. It's a careful balance of new learning, interaction, and keeping energy in the room. With concentration spans being more limited than ever, we have found that people need interaction every seven minutes in order to effectively interact with the content and see its practical application for their immediate world.

The return on investment for training consists of:

- Focus, where participants process selected content in a facilitated environment with clear and practical takeaways.
- Connection, where invitation to the training makes people feel special and leads to relational engagement.
- Identification, where the chance to engage with the broader leadership pool allows leaders to find candidates for future roles inside the organization or team.

Not all leaders are naturally great trainers, but those who intentionally work to become so, or invite strategic facilitators to help, can develop their people well.

One of our clients uses our GiANT toolkit as short training sessions with their team once a week before the start of their busy day. Training can happen in many ways and styles. Think of training as adding strength to your people. Help them get better.

Coaching

Coaching is the consistent investment in a small number of leaders over time with mutually agreed upon objectives, in an interactive learning process. This could look like one-to-one consulting, best practice core groups with a small group, or live troubleshooting.

The Liberating Others tool in Chapter 6 is a perfect way to coach others up. First, they need to know that you are for them. As a reminder, here are the coaching questions you can use to evaluate the needs:

1. What specific support and/or challenge do they need?
2. What is the tendency or pattern most undermining their influence?
3. How do you help them get to the next level?

Coaching is an ongoing, proactive process that must be intentional to see real results in those you lead.

Coaching can be so valuable for the 100X leader. Its benefits include:

- Depth, where personalized calibration of support and challenge develops higher personal performance.
- Collaboration, where the other person is learning from and with you—sharing best practices in real-life situations.
- Accountability, where actions get delivered. It is hard to hide from deliberate and personalized coaching.

Coaching well is a strength that leaders must perfect in order to be significant to others long term. The majority of adults can all be good at coaching but it takes time and practice to do it well.

Apprenticeship

Apprenticeship is a lost art in most places. It was once the norm in training up leaders, but has lost its importance with the proliferation of information available in today's world. It can still be found in the trades, as one leader shows another employee how to do practical, detailed work. Apprenticeship is the intentional transfer of knowledge, skills, and expertise into a person.

To apprentice is to invest long term in another person who has the capacity and desire to replicate skills and competencies. The return on investment includes:

- Capacity, where you raise up others to do what you do so that you can do other things needed in the organization.
- Scalability, where it allows the organization to grow because of the expansion of skillsets for the team or company.
- Influence expands, both for yourself and your apprentice, which strengthens the whole organization.

Here is a story of apprenticeship from one of our UK GiANT partners, Toby Bassford, who changed careers to become a consultant:

After a first career, I received valuable apprenticeship from Steve (Cockram) to become a GiANT leadership consultant. Here are just a few of the most helpful elements of that apprenticeship:

- There was a really clear and specific invitation up front— knowing what we were doing, what that involved, and that we were both fully committed was the best foundation. This wasn't just some generic fluffy occasional mentoring, this had a purpose and was a big deal for us both.
- Proximity. This has been a big deal for me. Being able to physically get a load of time together formally and informally

has been huge. It's meant I've seen Steve's thought processes, not just attended the structured meetings.

- Informal time together. I think this is where the real apprenticeship magic happens. It's chatting over a beer, debriefing on the train, being around last minute to attend a meeting, which is where you get some of the real insights.

- Steve has always made an effort to make phone calls when he has a moment – sometimes simply just to check in. Knowing that Steve has been engaged, interested, and available has been really important. It's also helped create a sense of permission to reach out to him when I've needed to.

- Opportunity. Steve has created genuine opportunities for me to "have a go" at something which has been so important, often slightly before I've thought I have been ready for it!

- Vision and encouragement. There have been timely and consistent reminders from Steve that he genuinely believes I can get there. There have been times when I actually didn't think I would, but Steve has never doubted (to me!) that he has known I would succeed. When I've wavered in my own self-belief, it's been great to rely on his belief in me.

Apprenticeship takes significant commitment on both sides. The cost/commitment on my part has been to move house and location to have a level of proximity to Steve to make it work. I wanted the best chance to learn and so my entire family moved so we could maximise time together—in meetings, over coffee/beer, delivering with clients, as much as I could. There's something about being together—watching, debriefing (especially in the informal times) that helps you really get under the skin of the person you're learning from. For me it wouldn't have worked without it.

Other things I've learned:

- You have to take the position of an apprentice. Get humble. Admit you're wrong. Show your weaknesses/vulnerabilities. You can only truly be apprenticed to the degree that you allow yourself to be!
- Being real and honest and getting past your own self-preservation has for me been one of the hardest things. Deliberately and intentionally saying, "I've no idea how to do this," or "I'm really finding this hard," or "I messed this up, can we talk about it?" These are the hard conversations.
- Sometimes at the beginning, you can feel like you are a spare part. Swallow the pride and play the long game.
- Three years has felt like a long time out of my depth in at the deep end. Fun at times, wearing at others. I regularly wondered if it was really worth the pain of feeling so consciously incompetent.

The end result is clear: I'm doing things I didn't think possible before. I am leading and influencing in contexts and with people at senior levels in organizations I never would have been without Steve's intentional investment over the last three years. I have greater capacity, am far more confident, and the world seems a far bigger place than it did before. I now see opportunities everywhere and believe it's all possible. I've also got a friend for life—the high and lows, challenges and encouragements of the journey have formed a relationship that will certainly stand the test of time.

Ranking Your Multiplication Preferences

All of us have different comfort levels and talents when it comes to the four multiplication methods. Steve's natural tendencies for multiplication are ranked as follows:

1. Training
2. Coaching
3. Apprenticeship
4. Informing

Jeremie's natural tendencies for multiplication are ranked as follows:

1. Informing
2. Coaching
3. Training
4. Apprenticeship

What about you? What are your natural tendencies for multiplication:

1. _____

2. _____

3. _____

4. _____

It is a conscious decision to learn to master the multiplication strategies that you are not naturally good at.

Which Method of Multiplying?

Each scenario below has a best-practice multiplication strategy to most effectively connect with others. Which multiplication strategy would you use for each of the following challenges—inform, train, coach or apprentice? (Answers at the end of the chapter.)

1. I want to communicate important information efficiently and accurately to the whole organization.
2. I need to raise up my successor in the next 12–24 months.
3. I want to share a vision of the future that will excite and inspire my people.
4. I wish I could get time to invest in and encourage my wider team rather than just my direct reports.
5. I need to drive performance higher for my immediate team and train them to think the way I do.
6. I need to grow my team so I can trust them to deliver for key clients even under extreme pressure.
7. I have so much expertise and wisdom I want to share but no time to do it.
8. I want to leave a legacy that lasts long after I'm gone.
9. I want to create a collaborative learning environment where best practices are shared.
10. I'd love to connect with the rising stars coming through our leadership pipeline.

Having reflected on the effectiveness of each multiplication strategy, now is a good time to build your own intentional transfer plan.

Intentional Transfer Plan

Consider what specific knowledge, skills, or expertise you need to transfer and to whom (see Figure 8.1). What leadership behaviors or wisdom need to be transferred to others?

Reflect on the tool shown in Figure 8.1

First, (and this might take a while) decide the Who. Are there up to three people in your life for whom you can create a plan to intentionally multiply your skills and expertise?

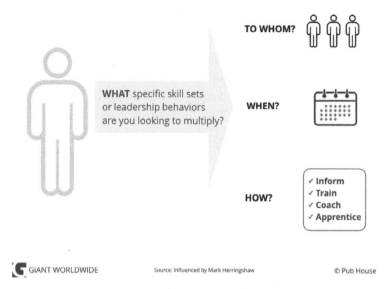

Figure 8.1 Developing an Intentional Transfer Plan
Source: © Pub House/GiANT Worldwide.

Are they on board? Decide what specific knowledge, skills, behavior, or expertise you want to multiply, when's the best time, and what is the most effective strategy for doing this, whether informing, training, coaching, or apprenticeship.

Taking the time to write out an intentional transfer plan is crucial for you to learn how to become a multiplication master, a 100X leader.

Here are some real examples of intentional transfer plans that we have used within GiANT that might help you in your world:

- **Mike Oppedahl (Apprenticeship)**—Years ago, Steve and I (Jeremie) put together an intentional transfer plan for how we needed to develop the managing partner of our GiANT Consulting group. We made a specific list—how we think about certain issues, the ability to grow the business, and so on. We used all four multiplication strategies to create a plan to transfer these skills to Mike, who was more than willing to learn. As the managing partner of our consulting company, Mike is now multi-plying himself into others on the team, and our appren-ticeship of him still takes place on a regular basis.

- **Hunter Hodge (Coaching and Apprenticeship)—** We have spent many years specifically coaching and apprenticing this keen young man, on creating e-mails, developing workbooks, and handling complex commu-nications. With a mix of support and challenge, he has helped us build out many of our programs including the 100X leader program (found on www.giant.tv). He has accepted every challenge with grace and now leads much of our training for GiANT.

- **Senior Consultants (Training)—**In our world, we are constantly working to train our senior consultants on the skills and expertise that are necessary for growing clients and dealing with the complex leadership, team, and culture issues that exist inside companies.

- **All Hands Meeting (Inform)—**From time to time we will ask everyone to meet with us from around the globe on a video call to inform on important matters. This process means that we communicate with clarity and conciseness.

Your world will doubtless be different. The key is to be *intentional* by building your plan for multiplication so that you can become a multiplication master.

Understanding Your Magic

Every one of us has learned a skill and gained wisdom or expertise that we could transfer intentionally to others. Your key employees, partners, and children could all benefit from you deciding to multiply your best into them. Yet no one will be able to leverage it unless we plan to intentionally transfer it. Here are some key questions for you to resolve:

- What is your magic? What do you find easy that others seem to find difficult? (unconscious competence)
- What specific knowledge, wisdom, skills, or expertise could you export to others?
- How are you multiplying it currently?
- How would it benefit you, your family, your team, or your organization if you multiplied your magic?
- What happens if you don't do anything?

Multiplication Kryptonite

We've given you many reasons and advantages of multiplying, but we have also learned from hundreds of leaders why they won't multiply. We call it multiplication kryptonite (the power that kept Superman down)—the true reason why you won't do something.

As you read through this list, circle the reasons you haven't chosen to multiply what you know to others and decide where your inhibition lies within each.

1. Where am I going to find the extra time to do all this?
2. Will I lose influence or even be replaced if I train others to do my job?
3. I really don't know what to intentionally transfer or to whom.
4. I am not sure I want to be that vulnerable with the people who work for me.
5. No one has done this for me, how can I now be expected do it for others?
6. What if I let people down and disappoint them when trying to multiply what I know?

7. Am I really prepared for such a long-term investment of my time and resources in the same people?
8. At this stage of my career I'm not sure I have the capacity or desire to learn so many new skills to intentionally transfer.
9. Do I really have any magic to multiply?
10. If I select favorites for coaching and apprenticeship, will the ones left out resent me and disengage?

Reflection on Multiplication

There is such value in the concept of multiplication. As we said earlier, the majority of leaders, when accidental, rarely multiply but, rather, spend most of their time subtracting, dividing, or—at best—adding. However, the really great leaders learn to multiply. They become competent in the four multiplication methodologies, all of which are important and need to be mastered to be a 100X leader.

To multiply is a skill set in and of itself. We have found that those who master it become outstanding organizational team leaders who understand the power of culture and how to excel at building teams at work, while expanding their influence at home.

Answers to Multiplication Strategy Test

1. Inform
2. Apprentice
3. Inform
4. Train
5. Coach
6. Coach
7. Train
8. Apprentice
9. Train
10. Train

SECTION
3

Creating 100X
Cultures

9

Creating the Atmosphere for Growth

You can't outsource culture! You must shape it, define it, and live it.

Although the Sherpa guides can't set the climate on Mount Everest, with its freezing temperatures and rapidly changing weather patterns, they can shape the atmosphere of their teams and the way things are done on the mountain from a leadership perspective. It takes work to establish and keep the healthy culture of any group of people, which is why there are so few leaders worth following in the world and why we need so many more.

We define culture as atmosphere. It is the air that people breathe while they are doing their work inside a team or organization. The leader defines the atmosphere by their style and standards. They shape it by their actions and reactions. They shape it by who they are and the work they've done on themselves to become leaders worth following.

Culture has many definitions. Our friend, author Ricardo González, says that the culture of a particular people group is defined by its language (or languages), beliefs, norms, symbols, and values.[1] He goes on to say that most of us are managing multiple cultures on a daily basis, including our family culture, our work culture, and our ethnic culture. There are thousands of rich cultures of people groups across the world. Each country, ethnicity, or organization has its own culture, and within the macro culture, there are even more subcultures.

Because culture is first and foremost about people and their personalities, most people have not taken the time together—as a family, team, or organization—to intentionally define it, share it, and grow the culture. It is very helpful though, for people to have a framework of values to share, not so that everyone will conform to a certain way of behaving, but because a commonly held framework grants the freedom to be true to themselves as well as providing a rallying cry to work for the good of each other.

We believe that, just like societal culture, organizational culture has vocabulary, norms, beliefs, standards, and symbols. In fact, one of our current fun projects at GiANT is to help a top American university create a cultural playbook for their athletic department. The leader understands how important culture is to the success of their work and they want to intentionally capture these norms, standards, and symbols so that they can spread effectively.

To shape culture a leader must first create a common language. Language is created through the establishment of a common vocabulary—words that come to mean the same thing, at the same time, with the same group of leaders. You can't create a common culture without the intentional creation of a common vocabulary. You'll have noticed much of the GiANT common vocabulary through this book so far, and our people all over the world share it.

This language can be used to positively shape culture because people use the objective language to communicate effectively, while getting things done. Peter Drucker famously quipped, "Culture eats strategy for breakfast,"[2] precisely because under pressure people revert to the culture at hand. You can see it in a sports team. If a team begins to lose you can immediately see the team's true culture. If players begin blaming each other or playing as individuals rather than a team, then any strategy will go by the wayside and the underlying culture (which the leader has allowed, for good or ill) will triumph.

When leaders use different vocabulary and language, they create their own silos. When everything is going well, no one notices. However, under pressure you end up with turf wars and culture clashes. Figure 9.1 shows the language components of a healthy culture.

The way you talk about your organization, speak to your people, and communicate with your colleagues makes a difference. Specificity and common understanding keep people on the same page, rather than trailing off to different conclusions based on everyone's own subjective perceptions. Therefore, consistency in organizational communication and cultural clarity depends on being able to clearly express your organization's culture strategy.

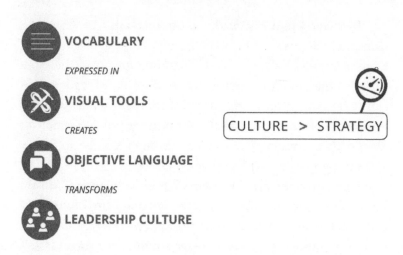

Figure 9.1   Language Components of a Healthy Culture
Source: **Susan S. Bean. © Pub House/GiANT Worldwide.**

This is precisely why mountain guides spend time drilling their climbers in a common language to use regarding their safety, roles, equipment, and time, so that everyone uses the same vocabulary. It saves time and can be vital in a crisis.

Does your team or organization have a common vocabulary? Is it objective or subjective?

All too often leaders are using their own vocabulary and language depending on what books they've read and what courses they've been to. This confuses teams and creates silos simply because of the language of a few.

Do you have a common vocabulary that is truly objective and helping you keep your vision, mission, and values in place? If not, we recommend that you use the tools in this book as a starting point.

Culture as Atmosphere

Culture is much bigger than ping-pong tables, restrooms, or parking policies. These, and multiple other things, are important elements of daily life within an organization but alone they don't make a firm foundation upon which to build the vision of the organization.

Culture is defined by the way the leader speaks to employees, the way they respond to challenges, or make decisions. Culture is the way that people are onboarded and the development that goes in to growing people. Culture is shaped by the values and vision and is reinforced by the consistency of relationships and communication. We believe the primary task of leaders inside their cultures is to keep the cross hairs of vision and values aligned. If you have a compelling vision and are winning but you aren't living your values, then in the end people will burn out and start to resent an all-consuming driven culture. On the other hand, a culture that focuses more heavily on values will always be a great place to work but will rarely deliver on its potential.

The metaphor we use to understand culture is the greenhouse, representing a team or an organization and the atmosphere inside it (see Figure 9.2). The gardener is the leader who must manage the atmosphere. Employees are the plants that need water, sunlight, and soil and are largely the responsibility of the gardener.

A greenhouse can be healthy, toxic, or out of control in the same way that teams and organizations can be. The health of a team depends on the health of the leader in the same way that the intentionality and experience of a gardener is vital to the health of the plants.

Figure 9.2   Culture can be understood as a greenhouse.
Source: **Photo used with kind permission from Annie Spratt/Stock image.**

Who Is Responsible?

We have observed so many leaders who recruit expensive talent and expect them to hit the ground running, but those leaders are then surprised that it doesn't work the way they envisaged. This accidental leadership would be similar to a gardener who buys the best plant she or he can afford, throws it in a dark corner and hopes it thrives.

Who is responsible for the growth of a plant, the gardener or the plant? We say both. The plant is designed to grow and wants to grow naturally. The intentional gardener would want a healthy plant, as well. Thus, both are responsible. In the same way, the employee and the leader are responsible for growth. They need to be planted in a healthy place, watered, and nurtured for longer than most leaders realize. They need to acclimate.

The 100X leader is the ultimate green thumb, or master gardener, because they choose to liberate and fight for the highest possible good of those they lead. The 100X leader intentionally creates a culture of empowerment and growth for their people and teams. It is an active process of calibrating support and challenge, always knowing what the other person needs and proactively providing it.

Here is a story from a leader working to create the right atmosphere for his teams.

As I visited with a principal recently, I was standing in the cafeteria of the school, which was full of students. The principal told me he realized that he's only in charge because the students allow him to be based on his influence. I feel this captures the essence of the Support-Challenge Matrix and the idea of building healthy cultures. We can only seek to influence others, not impose our wishes on them. I feel the Support-Challenge Matrix is much like Vygotsky's Zone of Proximal Development, which encourages teachers to provide students with opportunities to be challenged, but not overwhelmed. This nurturing is what is needed to grow leaders.

Over my 25 plus year career as an educational leader, I learned that it's my job to create a healthy atmosphere by training and developing others to do their work to their fullest potential. Leading by proclamation or intimidation is ineffective and leads to poor morale. On the other hand, failing to communicate high expectations and standards, leads to a lack of motivation and also poor morale. I work to try to educate, train, and develop those I lead. I am only in charge because they allow me to be and together we are growing into the leaders we have always wanted to be."

—Dr. Jeff Holm, Superintendent of Willmar Public Schools, Minnesota

Every leader is responsible for his or her growth. When we are growing, our influence expands. When we have influence, we can liberate others and help them grow. This is the essence of a 100X leader, who is acting like a gardener to those they lead.

Aristotle wrote, "We are what we repeatedly do."

The second part of that quote goes on to extrapolate, "Excellence, therefore, is not an act, but a habit."[3] Companies are no different. Whether they know it or not, organizations build culture around the things their employees and leaders repeatedly do and say. They are the result of daily habits throughout the organization, and, at the end of the day, the culture is being built. The only question is whether you are you doing it on purpose or by accident.

Though it sounds rhetorical, that question is actually quite serious and has real-life implications for the long-term health of your organization. Consequently, the following list of questions will help you begin thinking about how to purposefully shape your organization and cultivate the culture you truly want rather than the one you happen to stumble into:

1. How would you describe the current atmosphere of your team? Is it healthy or toxic?
2. Do you utilize a common language to help shape the culture?
3. How well do you think you balance the often-competing needs of vision and values?
4. Do you have a thorough process for raising new leaders?
5. How intentional are you in helping new employees integrate into your culture?
6. How do you celebrate together?

It's amazing what answering these simple questions can do to transform your organization from the inside out. So, take a moment to think about these realities, then gather the troops and start asking these questions. And don't be afraid to dive deep, you'll need clear language and common understanding if you hope to communicate effectively and generate the buy-in that will take you to the next level as an organization.

Toxic Culture?

If you were suddenly dropped on to Venus, how long would you live without a space suit? Maybe four or five minutes? How long would you be able to live in Dzerzinsk, Russia— known as one of the most polluted cities in the world? The average life span is a mere 45 years.

Atmosphere affects our breathing, which affects our work. If you're working in a toxic culture, then you may be experiencing manipulation by a dominating leader, which will affect your stress levels, your health, and your personal life. We will not thrive under dominating leadership in the same way that the plants will not thrive in the atmosphere shown in Figure 9.3. People need clean, crisp air to be able to work well. They need specific encouragement and they need a vision. We all need these things and your leadership either provides that or takes away. Some cultures can choke some people in a matter of minutes. Other cultures tend to kill people over months or years, causing gradual deterioration to an employee's well-being. The best cultures are free and clear and produce effective, long-term health.

So, what culture are you currently in?

What culture are you leading in each circle of influence?

Are you currently in the Venus atmosphere where you can't breathe for even one minute?

Figure 9.3 Nothing thrives in a toxic atmosphere.
Source: **Photo used with kind permission from Johnny Joo/ Stock image.**

Or are you in a smoggy atmosphere, where you know your health is declining over time?

Or do you thrive in an environment with clean air and plenty of sunshine in your culture?

Thinking of culture as atmosphere makes it easier to understand. In a city full of smog, it is possible to trace the cause back to specific political and business decisions or the geographic realities that allowed it to develop. You can actually follow the toxicity back to the ultimate source. So too can a toxic culture be traced back to a leader. Although this is not a witch-hunt, it is true that leaders affect the lives of everyone they lead by their words, actions, or lack of action.

Certain leadership decisions are built on short-term fear to produce results, and this can lead to a divisive culture, especially if the leader is more focused on vision (or profits) than values. As an employee, you can only rely on your influence to help clean up areas of leadership pollution. But if you are a leader, you have the opportunity to create an entirely healthy atmosphere for your people to live.

Toxic Realities

Do you want to see change in your culture? Would you like to improve the health of your organization and people? How about reducing turnover cost and improving efficiency?

If you answered yes to any of these questions, then a Columbia University study holds great insight and hope for you. A healthy company culture, the study shows, marks the key difference in employee retention and productivity. According to the research, organizations with rich company culture experience a mere 13.9% turnover rate, whereas the average job turnover in unhealthy company cultures reaches an astounding 48.4%.[4]

The reason for such disparity lies in the simple chain reaction of a poor company environment: unhappy employees rarely do more than the minimum, productive workers who feel underappreciated tend to quit, and poor managers adversely impact workers and their productivity.

Additionally, a study by Towers Perrin further detailed the stark difference between actively engaged and disengaged employees. According to the study results, companies with low levels of employee engagement suffered a 33% decrease in operating income coupled with an 11% decrease in earnings growth. On the other hand, companies generating high-level engagement produced a 19% increase in operating income as well as a 28% increase in earnings growth.[5]

The research is clear—healthy organizational culture matters. Not just for the heart of your company and its employees, but also for the bottom line. And the Sherpa is the key to getting employees engaged and getting to the highest levels.

Subculture, the Secret to Organizational Change

If you want to experience a culture overhaul, then there is a secret passage to do so. It starts at the subculture level. Since leaders define culture, the same is true of subculture leaders—they define subcultures.

What is a subculture? The answer is any team of people or division inside an organization that has influence. A subculture leader can be someone with influence but without a powerful title—maybe someone with years of experience who could be influencing a small group of employees because of their seniority. Or it could be a small division with well-established employees who like to do things their way. There might be a subculture of new employees or support staff, a group in the accounting department, a group that gathers for coffee, and so forth.

Each leader creates an atmosphere that other employees live in. In essence, each subculture leader is also a gardener inside the greenhouse that they tend. To be a green thumb is to liberate by assessing when the employees need more support or more challenge, helping them see the areas that are undermining their influence and helping them get to the next level. When you pair the Support-Challenge Matrix (see Figure 9.4 for a reminder) with the Leaders Define Culture tool, you can analyze your current sub-culture health and make some key decisions.

Now, look at your subculture leaders. What is their tendency? Do they tend to liberate, dominate, protect, or abdicate? Since leaders define the culture, then their influence will tend to shade the group that they lead, and that is how subcultures are built (see Figure 9.5).

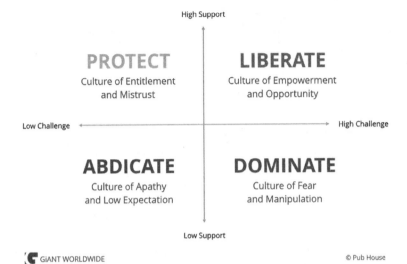

Figure 9.4   The Support-Challenge Matrix
Source: © Pub House/GiANT Worldwide.

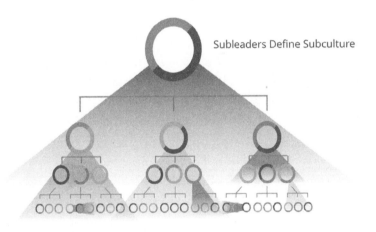

Figure 9.5   Leaders define cultures and subcultures.
Source: © Pub House/GiANT Worldwide.

Imagine what your subleaders will look like when plotted on the Support-Challenge Matrix. The subculture leader who dominates creates a toxic culture of manipulation and fear and while producing short-term results will most likely harm the effectiveness of their small team.

The protecting subculture leader will create a culture of entitlement and mistrust as they bring loads of support, but no clear expectations. Thus, challenge is seen as a negative, and the team carries on in whatever way they like. When the leader gets frustrated because of the pressure upon them, they can suddenly move to heavier challenge and cause mistrust because they are being inconsistent.

The abdicating leader can produce an apathetic subculture, because there is no support and no relative challenge. People are free to do what they like, and the culture is just gray.

Dominating or protecting or abdicating gardeners can create all types of atmospheric issues that won't allow the people to thrive or grow properly. They are not bringing liberation.

That is precisely why the subculture leader is the secret to overall culture change because subcultures are a culmination of the entire culture. If you want to change the culture you must change each subculture. If you are leading your organization, it starts with you and your senior team; you can't outsource culture. However, that isn't enough, you must also change each subculture. The subculture will be the primary experience of your employees.

After a recent conversation with a client, he mentioned that he was trying to make some decisions on whether to sell the business or keep it. Ideally, he wants to sell it to his employees, but they have been so busy running the day-to-day that he hasn't had time to effectively multiply. After the conversation, he finally seemed to realize that he must build up the subcultures to build a healthy culture enough to be successful once he was gone.

Manage the Subcultures or Lose the Entire Culture

If you don't manage the subculture you will lose the entire culture, and that takes years to get back. In fact, we believe it takes between two to three years to produce a true culture change because of the levels that must be reached to do it well. The larger your organization, the longer the process takes. This is why many leaders are tempted first to look for a silver bullet—"Surely HR can find a culture-building program we can roll out?!"

The truth is that historically most leader development happens to the top 15% inside an organization, and it rarely trickles down to the rest of the employees. We believe it's vital to impact as much of the culture as possible, and so we train organizations in multiplication by impacting 90% of the organization not just the top 15% (see Figure 9.6).

Figure 9.6 The Engagement Bell Curve shows how culture often develops versus how it should develop.
Source: © Pub House/GiANT Worldwide.

Usually, the top 15% (the executives) go on a course and start using ideas that they just heard but that aren't relatable or useful to the rest of the organization. It usually leads to resentment. The normal reaction is, "Just give them a few weeks and they'll forget everything they learned," which is usually true. Only by creating a multiplying language that everyone can learn and having a clear focus on the subculture leaders do you have the chance of creating a liberating culture, where 100X leaders are multiplied.

Are there any subcultures that are dominating your entire organization or team? Is there a department that is trying to be the hero of the company? Or is there an individual who is clearly out of line and dominating the flow of work or efficiency of a department because of their ego? These subcultures are not meant to rule the entire culture, but rather play their part in the growth and health of the entire organization. Most are unconsciously incompetent because no one has ever held a mirror up and helped them understand what it's really like to be on the other side of them. Tools such as these create an objective language that allow people to have the honest conversations that in many cases should have happened years ago.

If you are the leader of the organization, then it is your responsibility to support and challenge each subculture as you move forward for the greater good of the whole. If someone is out of line, then it is your role to get them either moving in the right direction or moving out the door. Liberating leaders challenge people to the agreed standards/values and the vision of the organization. If your culture is out of control, then it is up to you to lean in and deal with the situation with clarity, challenge, and proper perspective.

Sometimes, culture clashes occur because people are not supported correctly.

Other times, culture clashes need to be addressed head on with proper challenge.

Subcultures are not meant to dominate the entire culture, but rather help the organization to grow for the good of everyone.

> *Subcultures are meant to help the organization grow for the good of everyone*

If you want to be a 100X leader and lead an organization that everyone wants to work for, then it is imperative that you set the tone and create a culture that celebrates subcultures but does not allow them to lead the entire organization.

Transplanting People into Your Culture

Every growing organization hires new people, and those people are transplanted from one culture to another. In many ways it is similar to the process/technique of moving a plant from one location to another. Some organizations can focus so hard on their own greenhouses that they forget about the transplanting (onboarding) process.

Taylor Doe, founder of 3East.io, explains it like this:

In horticulture, transplants are used infrequently and carefully because they carry with them a significant risk of killing the plant. I see schools/organizations/businesses fire people too soon because "they aren't the right fit" when actually the organization(s) weren't careful enough in the transplant process. They didn't know the employee or athlete or student or their last greenhouse well enough for the transplant to be successful. I've seen the "death" of plants in companies happen too soon. The plants were actually potentially adding huge value, but the gardener gave up too soon. It was such a huge atmosphere change that it ultimately killed the plant because the master gardener wasn't patient enough or aware enough to grow the plant in the right ways. Each greenhouse is slightly different, and all plants react differently.

Goals for a Healthier Culture

You cannot change your destination overnight, but you can change your direction overnight.
—Jim Rohn

Just as Rome was not built in a day, neither will the organization or team you lead reach its ideal culture overnight. Progress and change take time, but reorienting your goals, adjusting your aim—that only takes a moment. And it's the recalibration of your trajectory that ultimately determines where you land.

Most leaders want to get better, but improvement happens when leaders start with clarifying vision and values together. When these are clear in every subculture, you have the beginnings of a solid foundation.

Knowing the challenge that lies ahead, the following are a couple of goals to consider for the journey.

Becoming Healthy

Although we generally understand what it means to be healthy physically, many of us find defining organizational health and care to be much more elusive. We know the steps to physical health, such as exercise, eating right, eating less, and so forth, but the key factors to organizational health are not as clear as we would like them to be. Although there are many potential answers to the question of effective indicators, Pat Lencioni provides a convincing summary of *cultural success factors* inside organizations in his book *The Advantage*:

- Minimal politics
- Minimal confusion
- High morale
- High productivity
- Low turnover[6]

The reality is that healthy things grow. If your organization is healthy then you will experience the growth that you have dreamed about. In order to achieve that, however, it is pivotal that you slow down enough to work on the cultural pieces that sustain a healthy, thriving organization.

To Be Productive

Productivity is more than working long hours and securing short-term financial results. Healthy people produce. It is that simple.

When we first started working with Ford Motor Company after the 2008 financial crisis they were asking vendor partners to help them create customer engagement so that they could turn the company around. We debated whether the focus should be on employee engagement first because customers become engaged to the degree that the employees are engaged. It made sense and they made the focus on getting employees engaged first, which drove production to significant financial highs.

Get the first part right and you are halfway there. Productivity usually occurs when people have a proper balance of support and challenge. However, when leaders create a culture of resourcing and equipping their people in conjunction with providing the appropriate challenge to encourage communication and alignment, productivity goes through the roof. As a leader, your example will set the tone.

Another word for productivity is *fruitfulness*—the concept that one seed can produce hundreds of fruits. That's influence at work within nature. So make multiplying influence the ultimate goal of both your leadership and organization to bear fruit in the lives of your team, family, organization, and community.

Culture Every Day

To be committed to becoming a 100X leader, then, you must be committed to the overall culture, starting with the subculture and seeking change from this level. Once you commit to being intentional with subculture leaders then you can use the tools in this book to help you build a liberating culture every day. When you decide to do this then you will most likely be on your way to becoming someone worth following.

Notes

1. Quote courtesy of Ricardo González, author of *The 6 Stages of Cultural Mastery* (Bilingual America, 2017).
2. "Culture eats strategy for breakfast" quote attributed to Peter Drucker and made famous by Mark Fields, president at Ford.
3. Aristotle, Book II of the *Nicomachean Ethics.*
4. Eliabet Medina, "Job Satisfaction and Employee Turnover Intention," (Master's thesis, Columbia University, 2012).
5. Source: Towers Perrin Engagement Gap Study (2007).
6. *The Advantage: Why Organizational Health Trumps Everything Else in Business* (J-B Lencioni Series, 2012), used courtesy of author Patrick M. Lencioni.

10 | Someone Worth Following

A Sherpa on Mount Everest has authority. Climbers listen to their Sherpas intently and respond to their instructions. Why? Because they have been to the top—the Sherpa know the mountain like the back of their hands, and the respect they have earned gains them influence. With this influence, the Sherpa responsibly and diligently guides their climbers, who are grateful, for without the Sherpa their chances of success are much smaller. The Sherpa are rightly revered and effectively lead people to make the right decisions in very challenging circumstances.

Climbers trust the competency of their Sherpa—their very lives are in their hands. Climbers trust their integrity, and they know it's not an ego issue. Because Sherpa have no personal agenda or need to win for their own glory, they are free to help people fulfill their potential and stay alive on the mountain.

We all need Sherpas in different times of our lives to help us get to the higher levels in our leadership journey. We need leaders who will not shirk from calling us up, nor will they abdicate when we need to climb harder. A few of us have been blessed to have a Sherpa at times in our lives, but most of us haven't, which is why we need more of the right kind of leaders in our world.

Sherpas are a prime example of leaders worth following. We simply need more examples—more people committed to fighting for the highest possible good of others.

Healthy cultures require this.

High performing teams thrive on it.

People desire it.

They desire the leadership that is hardly ever provided, only dreamed about. People want to follow people that are worth it. If you choose to be a 100X leader, then you are choosing to be someone worth following in the way that people want to follow someone they trust up the mountain. People want to follow someone who is secure, confident, and humble—someone who is leading others in the right direction.

On May 10–11, 1996, eight people died on Mount Everest in a violent storm. This disaster, which was captured in the *New York Times* bestseller *Into Thin Air* by Jon Krakauer, highlights leaders worth following and the relationships between the Sherpa, guides, and climbers.[1] To understand this in more depth, we reflected on Kate O'Keefe's work on the Sherpa mindset in her 2016 thesis, "The Mental Strategies of Elite Climbing Sherpas":[2]

Leadership was a strong recurring theme that highlighted the role of the Sherpa climbers whilst on expedition. In Kayes' (2004) study on organization disaster on Mt. Everest, documenting the 1996 disaster, a strong link was uncovered between leadership and learning. It was found that a direct leadership approach can both inhibit a team's learning but also be the element that determines life or death on Everest. In opposition to this study however, far from the narcissist is the Sherpa, and therefore climbing for personal glory and self-indulgence is not applicable. The 1996 Mt. Everest disaster was led by non-Sherpa Western climbers and therefore cannot compare to the Sherpas, and one can establish a clear link between the overpowering narcissistic doom that was placed on the expedition teams that day when their leaders were unable to make effective and life-saving decisions fogged by the temptation to reach the summit. In this study, the Sherpas highlighted that they are constantly checking the weather conditions, reassessing their goals and ultimately determining whether or not they will proceed. They also note however, that they work together as a team and without positive group rapport and effective teamwork, failure is imminent.

In *Everest*, the movie based on the incident, we see in more detail how leadership played a key role in this fateful 1996 disaster, as two different styles of guides worked feverishly to manage the different leadership styles of other teams on a crowded mountain in the worst of atmospheric environments.[3] Trust had not been established between the differing teams and the results were fateful for many. This lack of good leadership caused drama and chaos in the midst of high stress.

Climbing takes a coordinated effort of time, strategy, and resources. For the Sherpa, the responsibility of leading other people up a mountain while keeping their own stamina is understandably great. To guide others to summit requires outstanding levels of leadership and people skills.

Though our work places are not the summit of Mount Everest and it is most certain that 10% of your teammates will not perish on the leadership journey, it is evident that many adults do perish emotionally and mentally in their jobs, some languishing in the pit of despair for their whole career. As a 100X leader, your job is to create the environment where those you lead go far beyond anything they thought possible both as individuals and as a team.

Anyone who has led anyone understands the difficulties that come from asking a group of humans, with their own ideas of where they think the team should go, to join forces together and allow themselves to be led to accomplish something greater than they could do individually.

So, what is it like to be working for you? Are you easy to follow or difficult? Do you want to become someone who others willingly choose to follow? If so, that means first that you must establish both credibility and integrity.

Credibility Gap

Credibility is the quality of being trusted and believed in. What a gift it is to be truly believed in. This is primarily seen in competency. The more you prove your competency over time the more credible your opinions and influence will be. People trust what you say and value your insights and wisdom. They believe that what you say reflects reality.

Having credibility is one of the key components to establishing influence with others. It is possible to like a person without finding their views or insights credible!

To become someone worth following is to be trustworthy. But what happens when a leader loses credibility? How can that happen? Leaders are granted a certain measure of credibility with their team until they lose it. In essence, it is theirs to lose.

Leaders start to lose credibility when a gap appears between what they are describing and what the people listening to them know to be true. The CEO, speaking at the whole company meeting, is the ultimate acid test. When he or she describes company values—what they think the company stands for—you can see in the faces of those present whether there is a credibility gap.

Everyone knows the leader is a good person and truly believes what he or she is saying. However, the leader's experience doesn't relate to the reality the majority of the company is experiencing. It's obvious he or she doesn't know what it's really like for those on the front lines of the business. The employees know the CEO is sincere and means well, but they start to filter everything the CEO says through the credibility filter. They don't trust what the leader is saying to be actually true, and over time this undermines the CEO's influence.

This is when you hear phrases like, "Nice guy but he has no real idea of what is really happening on the front lines," or "If she would ever leave her ivory tower she might just learn a thing or two."

Here are some real-world examples of the loss of credibility:

An out-of-touch leader

The leader of a mid-sized company is highly charismatic. He loves the stage and grabs every opportunity to be on one. This particular CEO also loves to talk to clients and at industry conventions whenever possible. On one particular occasion, a group of employees was traveling with their leader to a trade show when they heard him say a few things about their company that caused them to be perplexed—he was talking about the company in a way that didn't match with their reality.

After the first comment, the employees just looked at each other with a shrug of the shoulders. After the third comment, they then started to roll their eyes. The CEO was exaggerating the size of their company and then some of their accomplishments. It caused the employees to wonder if he was lying or truly didn't know. In his defense they thought he really believed the information he was sharing was true.

The CEO lost some luster that day. A credibility gap began to open as his employees realized that he didn't actually know what was happening within the company.

A leader with a lack of attention

Susan had been overseeing the committee working on a special project for her company. She was a very busy executive and had built a strong team to work on this project. The problem was that because of her busyness she didn't spend the time or effort to obtain all the facts before she presented to the executive team. Her team would grow nervous because her lack of competency in reviewing the facts and making the case was causing a credibility gap. In the beginning, everyone knew of Susan's competency—she had a great reputation inside the company. However, that all changed when they began to work together, and they saw that her lack of attention to detail made the team look bad. The team liked Susan personally, but her lack of diligence caused a nervousness and a lack of trust that was well-founded once Susan presented to the executives. Because of this, Susan began to erode her credibility as a competent leader even though she was a likeable person.

All talk, no action

John and Linda were good parents to their three kids. They provided for their kids and had a good relationship with each of them. As their kids got a little older though, a gap started to open. John and Linda began to talk about things they would like to do with their kids. The problem was that they didn't do anything, they only ever talked about it. Their provisional ideas were seen as promises to their kids but when they didn't follow through, they were seen as broken promises.

Though the kids know their parents are genuine in their desire to do exciting things with them, they no longer believe they will ever happen. They may say, "Yes, sounds like a great idea Mom, we'd love to do that," but inside they have been let down before, so they have little expectation that it will actually happen. The credibility gap grows until the kids eventually filter everything their parents say through the lens of past disappointments. They know the parents mean well but the kids have limited or resigned expectations of follow through. A wide credibility gap can eventually lead to more distant relational dynamics, and the parents have no clue how it all started.

At the extreme end of the credibility gap is irrelevance. People begin to distrust the competence of a leader and therefore the leader's opinions and perspectives have little if any influence on decision-making.

When a credibility gap starts to occur, it is usually done unconsciously. Leaders rarely, if ever, know they have a credibility gap. It's not intentional. If it was, it would be an integrity issue and that's a completely different matter. You can rebuild credibility over time, but rebuilding integrity is significantly more complicated.

Losing credibility is one thing, losing integrity is even worse.

Integrity Gap

Integrity is the state of being whole and undivided. While credibility is hard to get back, integrity is almost impossible to recover once lost.

Losing integrity gets into character issues, whereas losing credibility touches on competency. Here are a few examples that can create integrity gaps and cause the plumb line of moral character to be affected.

At the end of every talk the speaker would wind himself up for a grand finale that included tears. His team would watch this occur at virtually every event. The crescendo and the tears definitely impacted the merchandise table—books would fly off the table with strong sales. At the end of the talk the speaker would say the same things as at the previous event. It sounded so convincing. The employees would eventually ask, "are those tears real? Is he a total fraud?" They questioned whether the well-timed tears were just manipulation to sell more books.

The Integrity Gap occurs when people believe someone is deliberately manipulating words and/or emotions to achieve their personal objective. Integrity is fundamentally about trust and intent.

The owner of a small business had a demanding presence. He had pushed the employees to grow the company at a record pace. As the company grew, so did the leader's appetite for finer things. The problem was that the owner was constantly saying that the business was struggling, and he began to ask his employees to accept pay cuts and salary freezes in order for the company to survive.

The employees began to look at the leader's lifestyle and started to question whether what he was saying was a deliberate attempt to make them work harder and accept lower pay or if the company was really in trouble. The integrity gap widened as the employees watched the owner buy a luxury car and a larger home at the same time that they were laying people off. Thoughts then became, "I don't trust you, I think you are lying so that you can maximize your profits for yourself." Ultimately, the owner's words didn't match reality and integrity was lost.

With a credibility gap, the leader and their opinions increasingly become irrelevant, because it is primarily a competency issue.

With an integrity gap, people don't trust what the leader is saying and why they are saying it, because it is fundamentally a character issue.

Credibility. Integrity. These are the areas where you want no gaps in your life.

It is hard enough to influence as it is. Leading is not easy in and of itself. Add in credibility or integrity gaps and it's impossible to become someone worth following.

The Everyday

Becoming a leader worth following is an everyday reality. It is the 365 days, 24/7 lifestyle at work and at home that must occur. It is not something that can be turned off or on like a light switch or something you just decide not to do one day. Everyone that you live and work with is observing your leadership every day.

These people are aware of who you are and the role that you play. They are looking for guides who are healthy themselves. They want people who add value to their lives, who take them to higher places and develop them. This is not an activity but, rather, it is the life they are living out.

This means that a 100X leader is an everyday lifestyle. Are you who you say you are? Are you really who people see you to be? It is the congruence of your words and your actions, not only in your team or inside the organization, but inside every circle—self, family, team, organization, and community. And, is that happening every day?

To be a 100X leader is a marathon, not a sprint. It takes a lifetime to build a reputation, but just minutes to destroy it! Every Sherpa, every guide, knows that being consistent is the key to safe climbing. The consistency of a Sherpa leads to trust.

> *It takes a lifetime to build a reputation, but just minutes to destroy it!*

Some of you are consistently excellent at leading in one circle. That might be the team or organization circle. The question is can you be the liberating leader in every circle, every day?

What would it look like for you to wake up in the morning and provide the proper support and challenge for yourself? This would mean that you are becoming a liberator to yourself.

What would your family and/or friends do if you were consistent, every day, within your family relationships or your key friendships?

The goal here is to begin to integrate support and challenge in every circle and to make sure your leadership in your team and work are as consistent as your leadership to your family and to yourself.

Eliminating the Gap

Every one of us has a chance to right our wrongs, to turn around and start to become someone worth following. It begins again at the start of each week—of each day.

We want to challenge you to constantly work on your "gaps." We are calling you to be intentional in every area of your lives and not allow your default tendencies or patterns to become harmful actions. This is incredibly hard to do, and we will all have moments where old patterns return, usually when we are tired or under some form of pressure.

Consistency over time is foundational to the 100X leader's influence; being honest and responsive when we get things wrong actually increases influence with others. Great leaders don't have days off where they become accidental because the stakes are too high.

It starts at home with the view of your family and/or friends.

It carries to your work, in every meeting you have.

You must eliminate gaps with every teammate and with every decision you make. It is the intentionality of your leadership that keeps you from credibility and integrity gaps.

Take a moment and think about the credibility gaps that you may have. Ask one of your trusted team members to tell you what gaps they see in you. Write them down and count this your opportunity to get to a higher level.

People Worth Following Bring Liberation

Being a liberator doesn't mean you're a perfect leader. We are human and will often be imperfect in our leadership attempts. Aiming for liberation, however, empowers you to hold up the mirror, take a hard look, and understand what it is like to be on the other side of your imperfections. How do others experience and view your leadership?

Using the Support-Challenge Matrix gives you a practical tool and a map to fight for empowerment and opportunity for those you lead and to give them the right support or challenge in the right situation at the right time. This leader in Canton, Ohio shares her experience:

After a season of reflection, I realize how much I have been losing credibility in my tendency to Protect inside my organization. The team I led was composed of both paid staff members and also an army of highly skilled volunteer leaders. After learning and applying the ideas from the Support-Challenge Matrix I realized that with the paid staff I led I was more capable of liberating leadership because I felt it reasonable to give them clear directives and expectations because they were being paid for particular roles. However, my tendency with our unpaid, but highly motivated and skilled volunteers was to protect them. I did a lot of the work for them, was passive in how I communicated expectations and offered much more support than was needed. The result was frustration for some people who weren't feeling useful enough and a few actually left my team to join other more exciting volunteer opportunities. In essence, I lost credibility because I over protected them, which was perplexing to realize.

When I became intentional in trying to become someone worth following, I began to deal with my tendencies and I started by communicating clearer roles with set expectations and deadlines for projects within the teams. I had held onto responsibilities myself simply because I didn't want to burden anyone else with menial tasks that I was perfectly capable of doing myself. Once I handed these off, my team felt empowered, trusted and motivated to work harder and go after a bigger vision of what could be. Instead of me coaching all our 100 + volunteer leaders, we established a team of seven coaches who led teams in their areas of expertise. We were able to increase the effectiveness of our training, apprenticing, and multiplying of our leaders because I wasn't the one doing everything. It also freed up my time as the Team Leader to spend more time looking ahead to a bigger vision instead of micromanaging details. My credibility started to increase, where I had been losing it.

—Suzi Lantz, Rivertree, Canton, Ohio

As Suzi shares her story, we bet many can relate to the tendencies she has shared. We have seen her change her mindset and style firsthand because people now really want to follow her, whereas, in the past, they may have done so just out of duty.

This was the story of work; however, Suzi is married with a family. Listen to her share from her personal life and how the 100X Tools and processes of GiANT have made a difference:

Within our marriage I realized that I was again a protector in every sense of the word. My husband has a demanding people-oriented job and even though my job is no less important, for some reason I've always felt compelled to bear most of the burden at home. I wanted to "protect" Jason from feeling too much stress and strain within our marriage, with the kids and our home maintenance so I adopted an "It's Fine" attitude. No matter what, I just dealt with it and said, "it's fine." Over time this developed over into a lack of any expectation for him to do anything at home and he began to abdicate simply because I was doing it all. I was resentful that he wasn't spontaneously helping me or proactively fixing things around the house. He's always been really involved with the kids, but as far as schoolwork, activities, transportation, etc., I had kept him out of the loop thinking I was protecting him from the stress of it all. Liberating leadership in my home has meant communicating much more clearly and establishing expectations and offering both support and challenge when things go undone. Simply giving my husband a blanket "pass" for not engaging in our household was very isolating to him and he actually developed resentment toward me because of it. Once we applied the Support-Challenge Matrix to this area of our lives and began to intentionally take steps to move in that direction our family life got so much better. We are going on regular dates together, taking weekends away, spending more time at family dinners and meaningful experiences with our kids, sharing the load of household responsibilities and really working as a team more effectively. It's been, in a word . . . liberating!"

This is the transformation that we desire for you. We want you to *become* someone worth following. We want you to *build* leaders worth following as you learn to multiply what you have learned, and we want you to *lead* teams and organizations that stand for liberation. We believe you can because we have seen so many people become 100X leaders and experience the liberation that we speak of here.

Why You're Never Quite Done Growing

Self-awareness, like climbing, is difficult.

Learning to hold up the mirror in front of ourselves and be brutally honest with what we see does not come naturally to most people. It is a necessary path however.

It will take time to walk through the process of self-discovery and self-awareness to help you see the potholes in your leadership and life that need to be addressed. We all have these issues—tendencies that lead to patterns of action that we face over and over again. We find ourselves saying things like, "Why do I always react that way?" and, "Why can't I ever seem to handle those situations better?"

Venturing into territory that we're not accustomed to is a new process of learning and trail blazing. We're not sure exactly where we are headed, or the precise path that will take us there, but we are determined to push through, nonetheless.

As we work through our tendencies and keep returning to the healthier path, a trail begins to appear under our feet, wearing a path that others around us can begin to see. Those ruts that we create over time are the tendencies that affect who we are and how we lead, for good or ill. Our lives are the sum total of the actions we take, most of which are based on the tendencies within us. Where we ultimately find ourselves can be traced back to the steps we took along the way.

Wouldn't it be great to be able to spot those tendencies ahead of time and catch and correct them before they result in negative actions? It's not a one-and-done exercise. Those tendencies/patterns are engrained in us due to who we are and the lives we've lived up to this point. Our paths as leaders are less about eliminating tendencies as much as recognizing and accounting for them.

We are never quite done with growing. This process of knowing and leading ourselves is a lifelong pursuit. We don't wake up one morning to finally realize, "I'm there! I don't have anything left to learn." There is always room for growth and improvement.

The journey is worth it, and the destination of a life-long pursuit of intentional growth is better than a life of accidental wandering. Every person who summits Mount Everest starts from base camp with an intentional goal. If you're not already walking, step onto the trail today and begin walking the path of becoming someone worth following.

The next and final chapter allows you to do a deep dive into who you really are. We lay out a step-by-step process that you can use consistently as you begin the process that can get you to 100X.

Notes

1. Jon Krakauer, *Into Thin Air* (Pan, 1997).
2. Kate O'Keefe, "The Mental Strategies of Elite Climbing Sherpas" (Master's thesis, University of Jyväskylä, 2016).
3. *Everest,* movie directed by Baltasar Kormákur (2015).

11 | The Sherpa Challenge

It's always further than it looks. It's always taller than it looks. And it's always harder than it looks.
—The three rules of mountaineering

The climb is always hard. The journey always long. In one moment you feel like you are on top of the world and then the headwinds hit you. This is just the way it is. We have never met a significant leader who hasn't missed a step or fallen down at one point or another. And that's just climbing on your own—it's even harder leading others up a mountain.

This quote from Mark Horrell puts the journey into perspective:

For the first 29 years of Everest's climbing history the death rate was 100%. Then Tenzing Norgay and Edmund Hillary climbed it in 1953 and came back down again. Suddenly the death rate was down to 50%, and it's been going down ever since.[1]

For some of you, the building of people while climbing yourself, feels daunting, tiring, and useless. People are just messy, work is hard, and expectations go unmet at times. Leading can feel like dying and to some degree it is. However, the more you experience the more realistic your expectations become.

Here is my (Jeremie's) story of dying and of starting to become a Sherpa:

It was 2012 and I was done. Since 2007 I had been leading the John Maxwell companies that we had bought and merged into GiANT. We had grown the Catalyst conferences into a national brand and successfully created a brand called Leadercast to become one of the largest leadership events in the world. We also had partnerships with significant thought leaders with the goal of changing the leadership landscape.

The problem was that as the leader, I was just dying. I was leading in what was my learned behavior, but not in my sweet spot. I was drained from work that was not life giving or energizing and drowning in detail. I was working on good projects that weren't satisfying my purpose or skills and so my mind was on the work more than on growing the people.

Steve and I decided that we would help coach each other as we were both dealing with some difficult things in each of our own worlds. During that time period I realized that my personality and my wiring were not designed to be as effective in the current role. We wrote more about this in our book *5 Voices* to help others understand how they are truly wired with their personality and how to become liberated and function more effectively.

Steve acted as a Sherpa to me and I realized that I was sinking under the weight of activities that were not in my natural strengths. He fought for my highest possible good in my job as I fought for his highest possible good in moving from the nonprofit world to being confident to leading in the business world.

Through that period of time I then began the arduous task of learning how to multiply my skills and expertise into others. The ongoing process of mastering multiplication does not come naturally to many, but it can be learned. Though I carry some scars along with stories of climbing and helping others climb to higher levels, I am still going after the higher levels myself.

All the tools we have created and shared in this book are from our experiences, and sometimes, our failures. What we have written comes directly from our real-life stories of climbing and multiplying. We want the highest good for you and can't wait to help you along the way.

Here is Steve's climbing story as it relates to becoming a 100X leader:

Just over a decade ago, my long-suffering wife and daughters moved with me from Yorkshire, England to Phoenix in Arizona. In total we were to spend five incredible years in the United States, two in Phoenix and three in a wonderful place called Pawleys Island in South Carolina.

Looking back, I realize that I had traded on talent, charisma and (debatable) charm for most of my life and never truly disciplined the talents I'd been given. This all changed when I arrived in the United States and started working for a highly charismatic leader. This leader constantly challenged me to become more intentional in every area of my life. He taught me how much could be achieved when natural talent was aligned with consistent discipline over an extended period of time. For some this boot camp experience would have finished them, for me it was exactly what I needed. I needed to be pushed.

I remember vividly a conversation at Starbucks that was particularly formative. I had become a healthier leader in every area of my life since arriving in the United States and had worked incredibly hard to master the content and methodology that underpinned our consulting business. The leader, acting as my Sherpa, told me that the next stage of my development was to decide what I wanted to be known for in 10 years' time. The natural answer for my personality type, who likes maximum influence with minimum responsibility, was to say, "world class communicator"! But deep down I knew that I would rather be known as someone who developed and apprenticed others. I didn't have the 100X leader vocabulary then but looking back this was instinctively what I wanted.

I remember inviting five leaders into a weekly coaching group with me after that Starbucks conversation and beginning to intentionally transfer what I knew into these five people. I think I learned more than they did but it was the start of what is now a foundational part of who I am.

Multiplication is far from glamorous. It's costly in terms of your time, talent, and treasure. It is an unseen commitment to support and challenge over an extended period of time, and there are no guarantees. Those we love and invest most in have the greatest potential to cause us joy and pain.

However, the fruits of multiplication are more rewarding than any public applause from a stage or dollars in your bank account. There is nothing like the pride of seeing someone you've invested in go on to do incredible things he or she didn't believe were possible. And, the fruit of multiplication lasts longer than you would imagine. People credit you over time with far more than you deserve. It's an investment that only grows over time as they forget how much challenge you had to bring to help them grow.

Ready to Climb

As you stand at base camp staring at a summit thousands of feet above, you can get spooked. Is this really worth it, you ask? The wind hits you as you step out of your tent. You are dressed and equipped. Your guides are rounding up the team, calling you up to steeper heights. It is time to climb.

Some of you will spend years climbing before you can lead others up the mountain. That is okay. The journey of 100X is actually the journey of being intentional—to wake you up from the accidental leadership that tends to lull people across the globe to sleep. You only get better when you practice, and we want you to start practicing climbing to 100% and once you are there, to start to practice the X—to multiply what you know to others.

There are great leaders who people want to follow, but the leaders' inability to multiply limits their influence and often frustrates those trying to follow them. Many well-known "gurus" fit these criteria as they have great wisdom and appear hugely influential through their writings and speaking, but they are not prepared for the incredibly hard, unglamorous yards of devoting their time, talent, and treasure to helping others climb. You want to follow the leader who is creating an atmosphere where people want to be, not where they're forced to be. The test is to look at the team and culture around them rather than their bank balance or possessions.

If you have made it this far in the book, we believe you want to become one of the servant heroes—a Sherpa, who liberates those they lead. Some of you have been longing to be a 100X leader, but you didn't have the resources or know how to start or even if you had it within you to do the hard work. It always takes longer than you think and is much more difficult to become a leader that someone actually wants to follow. It's time.

We have provided the tools and equipment you will need to climb, as well as given you a vision to be the best leader possible, while remaining healthy yourself in the process.

Plotting Your Course

It is important to understand the best way up the mountain. Do you really want to meander through life without a sense of purpose or direction? By bringing our unconscious tendencies, struggles, and frustrations to light, we can begin to address our underlying issues with intentionality and make tomorrow's version of ourselves a better one than today's. That is the mountain we must climb.

So how can you lead yourself better today in order to become the person you want to be tomorrow?

Whatever you expect of others, you must first expect of yourself. This cuts to the heart of leadership and influence. Leading yourself means having expectations for yourself, which means that all that you have learned from this book must begin in you first.

Why is this so difficult for leaders today? Most likely it's because we rarely talk about the need for leader consistency, nor do we often experience others who model the concept for us. Here are some areas you can apply to become a 100X leader:

- **Go deeper**—They say a tree grows up in direct proportion to the depths of its roots. If you want to truly climb to the top, then you must go to the core and build from the inside out.

- **Maintain inner health**—To get to 100% you must improve your spiritual, mental, and emotional maturity. If you are not healthy on the inside nothing can be healthy on the outside. Take time to recharge, rest, and center yourself each day, whatever that may mean for you. Many people have used our book, *5 Gears*, to help with how to be present and productive when there is never enough time. Remember, liberation begins with self.

- **Stay focused on the vision**—Remind yourself what you want and what your summit is because we all have different ones. Begin with the end in mind and create your map to the higher levels.

- **Live self-aware**—Be self-reflective in the morning, after lunch, and after dinner. To lead yourself means you must know yourself first. If others know you better than you know yourself, you are not ready for the top.

- **Leverage language**—Language sets culture. Leverage the positive by using the 100X tools you have learned to lead those in your world. Once they learn the objective language, they will begin to experience the same levels of growth they have seen in you.

- **Ask others to join you**—Make leadership a daily process. Get others involved. If you have focused on the preceding steps, you will see your leadership capacity and influence improve on a daily basis.
- **Fight for others best**—Let people know that you are for them by calibrating high support and high challenge for their best and begin to act like a Sherpa.

Becoming someone worth following is the 100%. There are plenty of leaders worth following who never choose to function as a Sherpa for others. This is the distinction between a 100 leader and a 100X leader, and 100 leaders often disappoint those they lead because for some reason they never multiply in the way they could. Their legacy is sadly less than it should have been.

100X leaders are incredibly rare. We want to help raise an army of them; leaders who have the capacity and desire to change the cultures of families, teams, organizations, and communities.

Choosing Your Guides

Getting healthy yourself is the first part of the climb. If you want to become a 100X leader, you need to be connected to leaders who are living that kind of life. That is what we do. We have multiplied GiANTs into Sherpas who are helping leaders summit.

We have laid out much for you to follow here, but the nuances of your real life need to be addressed for you to have the best chance of climbing the mountains ahead. We have also given you a path to climb at www.giant.tv to set out a clear process for your 100X leader journey.

We still believe the relationship with a coach, guide, consultant, or friend is most crucial to hold you accountable and get the best out of your leadership. We at GiANT are a resource, but there are also thousands of others who are qualified to help you in your journey to liberate yourself and others. The key is to find someone you trust, with credibility and integrity, whether a GiANT or another resource.

In the end, we simply hope that you will go for it—that you will climb the highest levels for your benefit and for those you lead in every circle of influence.

The Why

This book is not just leadership jargon but also a manifesto of what we truly believe the best leaders in the world to be. We became passionate about 100X leaders for personal reasons.

I (Steve) hadn't experienced much healthy multiplication, usually due to the insecurity of "legacy leaders" who always made it about themselves. True 100X leaders are humble. They don't seek the publicity or adulation of the crowds because their true reward will always be over a dinner with the individuals whose lives they changed forever, not holding them up as trophies but, rather, enjoying the quiet satisfaction of seeing others liberated.

This is the filter for those who are really ready to climb. For many leaders the lure of the spotlight is too great! We still struggle like everyone else with our own tendencies and insecurities, but we have set ourselves on a path and function as a group of

> *The Sherpa doesn't celebrate how many times they personally have been to the summit but how many times they help others get to the top.*

Sherpas constantly encouraging and challenging each other to keep going.

Remember, the Sherpa doesn't celebrate how many times they personally have been to the summit but how many times they help others get to the top.

My (Jeremie's) passion for 100X leaders came in the desire to be something that I had seen but hadn't fully experienced. In my early years I had benefited from a few amazing mentors who were truly 100X leaders and I wanted to be like them. But I have always found it difficult to have the patience or desire to truly multiply (X). Through some traumatic events, mixed with these good examples, I decided to become more intentional than accidental, which is not my natural personality trait. Truly, I struggle with both 100 and the X, but because I am committed to the climb, have worked hard on my gear, and have Sherpas around me, I continue the climb. That is all we are asking of you.

Your Turn

Our assumption is that many leaders will work on getting themselves healthy—shooting for 100%. A good few may start the early climb of multiplication but for those who want to function as true Sherpas—full 100X leaders—then in our experience there are three filters/questions that every person must address before the climb.

1. Are you prepared to deal with your own wall of self-preservation? Ask the three questions again.

    a. What are you afraid of losing?
    b. What are you trying to hide?
    c. What are you trying to prove and to whom?

2. What does success really look like for you? Is it about your name in lights or something even higher? If it's just about you, then you won't become a 100X leader.
3. Are you prepared to invest your life and talents in others with no guarantee of a return? Those we invest the most in have the greatest potential to cause us pain, but we believe the prize is worth the price.

Assuming you come through the tough questions, then it's time to quantify your reality. You need to be aware of your true starting point—to see what it is really like to be on the other side of you.

We have created an assessment for you to take to see where you are as a 100X leader. Simply go to www.100XLeader.com and take the 100X assessment.

You may not be thrilled with the results, but use it as a starting point to growth. If you want to become the best, then you must accept reality, plot your course, and create your game plan for liberation—for becoming a leader worth following.

The Reward of the 100X Life

The secure and mature leaders in this world have a "for others" more than "for ourselves" mentality. The rewards for living the 100X life are limitless:

- You will expand your influence further than you ever anticipated.
- You will have garnered the respect from those you lead in a healthy way.
- You will have created a legacy of which you and your family can be proud.

- You will get to see other people make different mistakes than you did as they climb to higher levels.
- You will receive the joys of having multiplied people and seeing their accomplishments benefit many.
- You will receive the gift of relationship as people will want to be around you.
- You will continue to grow yourself as you have adopted self-awareness as a guide of continual improvement.
- You will have more rest and peace in your heart and mind knowing that you are leading in the best way possible.

Living for others and leading from a place of health is truly remarkable. It is not idealistic, but entirely feasible. You will simply need to make some decisions. First, are you willing to go for it? Second, do you have the right equipment? Third, do you have the right guides?

Since you only live once, wouldn't living as a Sherpa be worth the try? There is peace and joy and freedom in this style of leading, even amid the many hard days and frustrations that come by serving people and pushing them to higher levels.

We encourage you to not miss the opportunity to see the incredible views when you help others summit.

Sherpa Challenge

There are just too few leaders who are willing to give themselves to help others get better. Some call this servant leadership, but we think it's even more than that. Yes, a Sherpa serves, but they also fight. That is the beauty of liberation. A

The true legacy of a leader is not how many times they have reached the top, but how many times they have helped others reach the higher levels.

liberating leader does both, serves and fights, because both are needed.

A 100X leader will leave a legacy because liberating leaders become significant and memorable in the lives of those they lead. Remember, true legacy of a leader is not how many times they have reached the top, but how many times they have helped others reach the higher levels.

This is a good time to do something for those who have been liberators to you. Take a moment and write a letter or note to someone who has been a Sherpa to you and share specific instances that helped you reach higher. Thank them either in person or in writing and tell them why you are doing it.

And, commit to becoming a Sherpa for others.

At the end of the day, there must be no excuses or regrets. You have a mountain to climb and there is a mountain that you can help others climb.

May you be one that sets a new trajectory for you and for those you lead. And, may you celebrate the summits of those you lead and train them to do the same. When we do that together, we just might create the plan that changes cultures around the world.

Don't wait to liberate yourself and lead yourself to heights you once thought unimaginable. Do it.

Don't wait to dream higher for people and hold them accountable to their own dreams. Help them.

Don't wait to calibrate high support and high challenge for others. Learn how to lead more effectively.

Don't wait to create the culture of empowerment and growth. Help the subculture leaders.

Don't wait to give something away to someone who needs it. Resource them.

Don't wait to call people up, not out, as you help them see an area of growth in their life. That is how people mature.

Don't wait to give more of yourself to family, friends, and colleagues. When you give it away you get far more in return.

Please don't wait to bring life in a world that is full of chaos. People need you!

This is the Sherpa challenge and why the analogy is so powerful. The Sherpa are worth following because of their skills, expertise, and professionalism. And even more because their humility means their true success is not about them, it's about those they help climb.

Fight for the highest possible good of those you lead—live as a 100X leader!

Note

1. Mark Horrell, mountaineer and writer, www.markhorrell.com (blog).

Our Gift to You

The book is over, but the journey has just begun. As a faithful reader who made it to the end of this book, are you ready for your free gift? It's something that's been specifically designed to help you lead yourself and others up the mountain of work and family and life.

We want to give you a free month of access to GiANT TV. What is GiANT TV? It's like Netflix for 100X leaders. GiANT TV is a media platform where we upload our premium teaching content (the same content that we teach at companies like Pfizer, Google, and other Fortune 500 companies), and it can be streamed to almost any device.

A book can only teach so much due to the space restrictions of the physical page, but GiANT TV can go much deeper into the concepts introduced here. To get your free month of GiANT TV simply visit:

http://www.giant.tv/freegift

It has been our privilege to be your Sherpas, but we know how easy it would be to put this book on a shelf and allow your excitement to die down. Please don't. Instead, use Giant TV to continue your transformation into a 100X Leader.

Let's all work to get to the next level!

Sincerely,

Jeremie Kubicek and
Steve Cockram

Acknowledgments

We have a bevy of people to thank for their outstanding help with the writing of this book.

We want to thank Helen Cockram for her editing and for her eye for ensuring that our intent matches our words. Your work has made us better. Thank you.

We couldn't be prouder to serve leaders around the world with the GiANT HQ team—Mike Oppedahl, Brian Fletcher, Hunter Hodge, Amy Ferguson, Connelly Rader, Justin Westbrooks, Rich Webb, Jared Humphries, Tracy Rader, and Emily Humphreys. Thanks for working so hard on the guts of our old and new businesses and allowing us to do this important work.

To our partners, senior consultants, ambassadors, internal Sherpas, and certified GiANT coaches, we are inspired by your hunger to want to liberate leaders across the globe and consider it an honor to work together with each of you.

And to our literary agent, John Willig, and our publisher and team at Wiley, thank you for believing in our mission. We are just getting started!

To Tracy Rader and Jessica Rimmer, thanks to your extra eye and great feedback on the review. Super helpful. Appreciate you taking the time you did to help so many.

From Jeremie

I am so incredibly grateful to my wife, Kelly, for her partnership in marriage and for her patience with the writing process. You are a true GiANT. Thanks for liberating our family and for your influence on so many. I love you!

Special thanks to my kids, Addison, Will, and Kate. Thank you for putting up with so many writing seasons. You inspire me and make me so proud for who you are as people. I am so excited to see how you continue to practice these principles for the rest of your life.

I can't speak highly enough for my business partner and friend, Steve Cockram. You are the real deal—a true 100X leader. Thank you for calling me up consistently and for believing in my voice. It is so fun running the business together and bantering back and forth on the Liberator Podcast. Can't wait for what is next.

Grateful for my GiANT partner pack and our HQ team—thank you for liberating leaders and working so hard for so many!

Special shout-out to all who have served in the writing of this book in big and little ways. To Mary Myrick, for allowing me to have some amazing views to write from at Carlton Landing and to Tony Yacovetti for the perfect hideaway in Florida to finish the last bits. Thank you!

Thanks to you Mike and Kianna Kubicek for being 100X parents. Thanks for pouring in to us so we can pour in to others. You are the best!

And, to the clients I call friends, who allow me to be me to help you be you. Thanks for allowing me to be a Sherpa to you through the years and in some cases decades.

From Steve

My thanks go to those people who have been a 100X leader to me, notably Graham Tomlin, Roger Sutton, John Lovell, and Mike Breen. I will always be grateful for the incredible investment you made in my life.

I would like to thank those who, a decade ago, gave me the opportunity to take my first faltering steps as a Sherpa—Armandee Drew, Brandon Schaefer, James Warren, Doug Paul, and Grant Eckhart. And my thanks to all those who have allowed me to play a Sherpa role since then—I'm so proud of all you have achieved and are now multiplying into others—Eric Pfeiffer, Toby Bassford, Jane Fardon, Mike Oppedahl, Terry O'Regan, John Cotterell, Matthew Kimpton-Smith, Keith Style, Jason and Suzie Lantz, Graham and Rachel Hawley.

To our dear friends Frog and Amy Orr-Ewing and the Latimer Minister community for their constant encouragement.

To Jeremie Kubicek, a true 100X leader. Your energy, intentionality, and passion for liberation are an inspiration to me and the whole of our GiANT family. You have carried by far the greater share of writing this book—thank you for expressing us so well.

To my parents Ian and Sue Cockram, the most supportive and liberating parents anyone could wish for. And finally, to my beloved wife Helen and daughters, Izzy, Megan, and Charlotte—you inspire and liberate me every day to do what I love. Thank you.

About the Authors

Jeremie Kubicek is a thought leader who specializes in unlocking leaders and getting them to a higher level through his speaking, coaching, and writing. Jeremie has the unique ability of taking complex concepts and turning them into powerful tools that are practical and scalable for individuals and organizations. As CEO and cofounder of GiANT, he oversees the licensing and digital platform, GiANT.tv, to help people around the world receive powerful and inspiring content.

In addition, Jeremie is the former CEO of Leadercast and the Catalyst conferences and a best-selling author of the book *Making Your Leadership Come Alive.*

Together with Steve Cockram, he also has written *5 Gears: How to Be Present and Productive When There Is Never Enough Time; 5 Voices: How to Communicate with Everyone You Lead;* and now *The 100X Leader.*

Steve Cockram is an international speaker, author, and consultant to top-level executives and leaders around the world. He is a subject-matter expert on personality and wiring, organizational leadership, emotional intelligence, and interpersonal communication. As cofounder of GiANT Worldwide, Steve influences the GiANT consultants and works on content, from the 5 Voices leadership system to original content at www.GiANT.tv

About GiANT
Worldwide

GiANT is a content development company, specializing in leadership transformation. With a consulting division of professionals working in over 15 countries; a licensing division of the powerful 5 Voices system and the digital media platform, GiANT.tv, GiANT produces scalable and practical content and programs for people wanting to be relevant in the twenty-first century. The leadership language of GiANT is being used in organizations, large and small, to change the way people lead.

Our specialties include:

- Teaching a common language that 90% of an organization can understand, use, and teach.
- Utilizing visual tools that shape culture and enhance leadership growth.
- Inserting a pass-it-on apprenticeship process into organizations that blows away traditional leadership development programs with a system that impacts culture for a decade.
- Focusing on individual transformation rather than on information transfer. We teach self-awareness that spreads

throughout teams to produce secure, confident, and humble leaders.

- Serving clients in agile and relevant ways to fit the fast-paced, task-oriented work world.

To find out how to powerfully grow your leaders, teams, and organizations or to see how to become a part of GiANT as a senior consultant, license specialist, or joint venture partner go to www.giantworldwide.com.

Speaking Inquiries for Jeremie Kubicek and Steve Cockram

If you have enjoyed the content created by Jeremie Kubicek and Steve Cockram and would like to bring one or both of them to speak at your conference, organization or event, you can contact them at:

www.jeremiekubicek.com
www.stevecockram.com
www.giantworldwide.com/speaking

Topics include:

- 100X Leader: How to Become Someone Worth Following
- 5 Voices: How to Discover Your Voice, Build Your Team, and Change Your World

- 5 Gears: How to Be Present and Productive When There Is Never Enough Time
- Making Your Leadership Come Alive
- And much more

Index